STUDENT-FRIENDLY GUIDES

STUDENT-FRIENDLY GUIDES

Preparing for traditional exams
for undergraduates and taught postgraduates

PETER LEVIN

Open University Press

Open University Press
McGraw-Hill Education
McGraw-Hill House
Shoppenhangers Road
Maidenhead
Berkshire
England
SL6 2QL

email: enquiries@openup.co.uk
world wide web: www.openup.co.uk

and Two Penn Plaza, New York, NY 10121-2289, USA

First published 2004

A catalogue record of this book is available from the British Library

ISBN 0 335 21576 9

Library of Congress Cataloging-in-Publication Data
CIP data applied for

Typeset by YHT Ltd, London
Printed in the UK by Bell & Bain Ltd, Glasgow

Contents

List of Checklists vii

List of Boxes viii

The strange world of university examinations. READ THIS FIRST! 1

Introduction 5

Part One: Using past exam papers

Get hold of past exam papers 13

What to look for in past exam papers 16

Unfair questions 21

The guessing game: what topics will come up this year? 25

Part Two: Formulating model answers

Interpreting the question 31

Methodology 35

Materials 42

Drawing up a plan 45

An alternative approach: the 'question string' 50

Choose your introduction 53

Argument or chain of reasoning? 56

Writing exam answers: some more suggestions 58

Questions for examiners 61

Part Three: In the run-up to exams

Revising effectively 65

Memorizing 69

Make best use of your time 75

Getting in the right frame of mind for exams 80

Part Four: On the day of the exam
Be organized 91

Further reading 99

Acknowledgments 100

List of Checklists

Checklist 1: Examination practices 9

Checklist 2: Past exam papers 14

Checklist 3: Question types 17

Checklist 4: The language of exam questions 18

Checklist 5: Unfair questions 22

Checklist 6: Guessing this year's topics 26

Checklist 7: Interpreting the question 32

Checklist 8: Methodology 38

Checklist 9: Materials 43

Checklist 10: Points to cover in drawing up a plan 46

List of Boxes

Box 1: What exactly *is* an exam question? 15

Box 2: What examiners are looking for 27

Box 3: If you have a disability 62

Box 4: Make good use of revision sessions 68

Box 5: If you become ill or there's a family emergency 74

Box 6: Avoid getting wound up by other students! 78

Box 7: Practise writing legibly 78

Box 8: Get the sleep you need 87

Box 9: After it's all over 97

Box 10: Web links, feedback, updates 98

The strange world of university examinations

READ THIS FIRST!

The world of the university – the 'academic world' – is a world of its own. It's very different from the 'real world' in which you and I and most other people exist. If you're a student, you must have become aware that the academic world is a world of 'mental constructs': descriptions, theories and explanations, ideas and critiques. You are expected to get these into your head through the medium of – in particular – the written word and the spoken word, via books and articles and web pages, and the lectures that academics give. So in the academic world you're learning at second hand, so to speak, rather than through your own experience, as you do in the real world. Learning at second hand does not come naturally to most people. You need some help. Sadly, such help is in short supply in the academic world. This book, like the others in this series of student-friendly guides, is designed to fill that gap.

Not only are there differences in ways of learning between the academic world and the real world. There are differences in how you and your learning are put to the test. In the academic world, the great majority of students are faced with – *examinations*!!!

There are several different methods of assessment employed in universities in the English-speaking world, but the traditional, 'unseen', examination is still dominant. You go into an exam room, without any books or photocopies or notes, sit down at the desk allocated to you, and find in front of you a sheet (or several sheets) of paper with questions printed on it. This is the exam paper. You spend two or three hours writing in an 'answer book' your answers to some or all of these questions. When the invigilator calls out that time is up, the exam is over. You stop writing, get up and leave. A few weeks later, you discover what mark you have been given, and – if you have been taking your final exams – what class of degree you have been awarded.

Like all traditions, unseen exams have their bizarre features. In essay-based subjects in particular, many of the so-called 'questions' aren't questions at all: that is, they aren't direct questions, interrogative sentences with a question-mark [?] at the end. Instead, they are instructions: 'Analyse ...', 'Compare and contrast ...' Another common instruction is 'Discuss.' You think 'discuss' means having a conversation with someone else? Not here! In exams you have to discuss on your own.

Most university courses change little from year to year. But every exam has to have questions that are different from those of last year's exam and those of the few years before that, otherwise students would be able to turn up to exams with prepared answers. So every year the examiners who set the exam paper have to invent new questions. Sometimes this is done by remodelling past questions – a direct question one year is transformed the following year into a statement to be discussed – but very often it is done by inventing complications, especially new wording. Given that every academic subject already has its own version of the English language – I call it 'academic-speak' – this requires students to develop a very particular exam skill, that of *interpreting* exam questions. Needless to say, very few – if any – academics teach their students this skill. (If you're an international student, please note the widespread use academics make of synonyms. English usage today does not favour the repetition of words: which is why I used the word 'transformed' instead of 'remodelled' earlier in this paragraph.)

In the run-up to exams you'll also be on the receiving end of some mixed messages. (Nothing new here!) The fact that you can't take any books, photocopies or notes into the exam room with you may give you the impression that exams are memory tests. But almost certainly your teachers will say to you something like this: 'Exams are not memory tests. We don't want our lecture notes regurgitated. And prepared answers will be penalized.'

At exam time your teachers become your assessors. They may not find this dual role an easy one. On the one hand, they want you to do well. (Could be they're fond of you; could be they're aware that poor results reflect badly on their teaching.) On the other hand, they want to uphold the standard of their degree, and they can't afford to risk attracting adverse comments from the 'external' examiner, who will be from another university. So one day you may find them being surprisingly helpful; another day you may feel you're being treated like an artful dodger on the look-out for ways of cheating the system. Indeed, you may experience the relationship with your teachers as a kind of game, in which you have to work out for yourself what the rules are for winning: what the examiners' expectations are, what approach, style etc. will be rewarded and what will be penalized.

In this book, like others in this series, my aim is to help you to take control of your situation: to 'read' the system, to 'suss out' what's going on, to develop skills like that of interpreting exam questions and constructing answers, to cope with the stress that inevitably accompanies exams, and to be confident in what you're doing. To this end I have done my best to demystify the traditional exam system, to address the many issues which students raise, and to suggest practical courses of action. I've tried to write in plain English, and to help you to deal with academic-speak. Whether you've come to university from school or FE college, or you're a mature student or an international student, I hope this and the other guides will help you to master and enjoy your studies, and to win the qualification you're after.

Peter Levin

Introduction

Many university examinations are of the traditional, 'unseen' type: you have two or three hours or so to answer a number of questions which you haven't seen before, and you aren't allowed to take any books or notes into the exam room with you. My purpose in writing this book is to help you prepare for such exams, especially those that require you to write essays.

I also aim to answer some frequently asked questions, such as these:

- I've looked at past exam papers and I'm really confused: what are the examiners looking for?
- I haven't taken exams like these before: how should I prepare for them?
- What does 'Discuss' on an exam paper mean? Discuss with whom? What am I supposed to do?
- I get good grades for my essays during the year, and then poor marks in examinations. What am I doing wrong?
- I have these long reading lists for my courses: I simply can't read everything on every subject we've covered during the year. What can I do?
- I've made this great pile of notes during the year: should I try to condense them?
- Other students seem much better prepared than me and to work much longer hours. It's very discouraging. How can I keep my motivation up?

In writing this book I have been guided by certain principles.

First, your teachers owe it to you to make it clear to you what is expected of you, in particular what you need to do to get a First, Upper Second etc. Unfortunately it is often the case that expectations are not voluntarily made explicit to students. And because different teachers and departments have different expectations of students, it is not possible for me to be an expert in all of them. So my approach in this book is to offer you suggestions as to how you can go about eliciting this information for yourself, from your own teachers and from reading between the lines of the exam papers they set.

Second, I recognize that different people have different aptitudes, different ways of learning, and different styles of working. Various bits of advice in this book suit many people (they have been tried and tested) but it would be surprising if they suited everyone. You may already have your own methods that work reasonably well for you and that you don't want to abandon: it is not my aim to change you. So please treat the advice in this book as suggestions, not instructions.

Third, in almost all university courses, two kinds of learning are on offer. At one level, and most obviously, you learn the subject matter. But in addition, at a deeper level, you have the chance to learn how practitioners of your subject think, how their minds work.

Thus, If you're taking a law course, you can learn the law – but you can also learn how (English) lawyers think. Likewise you have the chance to learn how economists, geographers, anthropologists, whoever ... think: how they see the world and their subjects, what registers with them, what kinds of reasoning they habitually employ, and so on.

Arguably, the difference between an Upper Second and a Lower Second is that if you show you have learned to think in the way that your teachers think, you get an Upper Second; if you haven't managed this, you won't do better than a Lower. So in the course of writing this book I've tried to help you to understand how your teachers think, and to write with them in mind. I do this by paying attention to the language they use in framing exam questions and to the methodology you can use in writing exam answers, and by concentrating on offering you a systematic way of working under the pressure of a time limit.

My fourth principle arises out of another twofold distinction that you should be aware of. In the experience of most of us there are two kinds of writing. On one hand, there is 'writing as thinking', part of the process of 'puzzling things out', making sense of them. Writing as thinking is usually a slow process, not least because it involves a lot of drafting and redrafting and looking up and checking your sources. On the other hand, there is 'writing as assembly job'. This comes into play when your thoughts are already well formed in your head and all you have to do is to assemble them on the paper in front of you. 'Writing as assembly job' is much faster than 'writing as thinking'.

An exam isn't the place for thinking your subject out on paper; there isn't time. (What you *must* think about during the exam is how to structure your answers.) So my fourth principle is that I can best help you by showing you how you can treat the actual writing of your answers in an exam as an assembly job.

Finally, you yourself bring ways of learning with you when you come to university. Not only do you learn by 'studying', by following the curriculum: your whole life has been spent learning – by imitating other people, by trial and error, by practising over and over, by putting two and two together, and especially by 'sussing out' how systems work. Although there is a major difference between such 'experiential' learning – learning from your own experience – and 'book/lecture-based' academic learning, it clearly makes sense to use your experiential learning skills as much as you can in preparing for tackling traditional exams, and so my fifth and final principle is that I should wherever possible help you to use these skills rather than ignore them.

In the following sections I draw on these principles in suggesting practical techniques for preparing for traditional exams. They are all techniques that have been tried out and reported on by the hundreds of students with whom I have worked in the past four years.

I'd like to conclude this introduction with some thoughts on the continued use today of traditional, unseen exams. Some people regard them as an obsolete method of testing ability, and several alternative methods have been developed. A well-known system is continuous assessment, whereby students take a test every week or two. On some courses you have to submit essays or other pieces of homework at less frequent intervals, and these are assessed and count towards your mark for the course. In some places you have to sit an end-of-year exam where you are given three or four hours to write just one essay. Why do some universities persist with unseen exams, in a tradition dating back a century or more?

First, this system makes for fair and impartial assessment. All students take their examinations under the same conditions. There is minimal possibility of plagiarism or of work being submitted that has been written by someone else. There is a well-established marking system.

Second, there is no system of assessment which does not create pressures on students. With unseen examinations in the Summer term or at the end of a semester, you know exactly where and when the pressures will come.

Likewise you know exactly when it is that you will *not* be under examination pressures.

Third, most courses 'build' through the year or semester. Although teaching is often structured around a sequence of topics, these are rarely discrete: they don't fall into self-contained 'compartments'. For example, under the three-term system, a topic covered towards the end of the Spring term may well be related to topics that you covered in the Autumn (Fall) term; you may find that a methodology introduced in March can be applied to a subject you worked on in the previous November. And your Summer term classes (especially 'revision classes') will provide an opportunity for an overview of your course and for you to notice interconnections and overlaps and how everything comes together. All this makes the end of the academic year the appropriate time for assessment.

If you're faced with end-of-year or end-of-semester traditional exams, my suggestion is: *make the most of it!* For the two-thirds of the year or semester when exams aren't in the offing, you are free to concentrate on *learning*. And at those times teachers are not forced to take on the role of assessor. They have more freedom as teachers. This is valuable because the roles of teacher and assessor do not fit comfortably together. To be an objective and impartial assessor it is necessary to hold students at a certain distance; to be a good teacher it is necessary to be reasonably close to your students, at the very least to be able to put yourself in the position of a student who is grappling with a difficult task.

What are the implications of all this for you? You have certain resources and certain opportunities. Towards the end of your courses you will have acquired for each of your courses a stack of lecture notes and handouts, notes made in classes, tutorials or seminars, essays with marks and comments from your teachers, marked homework in the case of quantitative subjects, books, papers and photocopies with passages marked and highlighted, and sets of past examination papers.

In addition to possessing all this material, if you have attended lectures and classes/seminars regularly you will inevitably have soaked up something of the subject without necessarily realizing it. As for opportunities, there should be a period of time between the end of teaching and the beginning of exams which you can use for revision and review, for consolidating your work, and for seeking help from your teachers. This book is dedicated to helping you to make the most of this time.

It's never too early, however, to ask how the system works in practice. So, to end this Introduction, here is a checklist of questions to ask your teachers, if they don't volunteer the information to you first:

Checklist 1: Examination practices

Are exam scripts (answer books) submitted and marked anonymously? Are the candidates' numbers randomized? Are scripts marked independently and 'blind' by two examiners, i.e. the second doesn't know what mark the first has given?	These are important precautions against the possibility of witting or unwitting prejudice in marking.
Are scripts over which there is disagreement or which are borderline sent as a matter of course to be scrutinized by an external examiner?	The external, impartial scrutineer provides a further defence against prejudice, besides helping to ensure that the standard of the degree is upheld.
Is there special provision for people who have a disability?	For example, anyone who has been given extra time for the exam should be able to take it in a separate room where they won't be disturbed by other people leaving when their own time is up.
Is there a fixed quota of Firsts, Upper Seconds (or Distinctions, Merits) etc?	If this is the case, you need to be aware of it. It's a very unpleasant system, because it forces students to compete with one another.

Part One

Using past exam papers

Get hold of past exam papers

Past exam papers are a hugely important and valuable resource for you. Try to get hold of the past three years' papers for each of your subjects. (Four may be better; from five they may be getting out of date.) And spend some time going over them until you are really familiar with them.

You can use past exam papers for many purposes. The most obvious – and crudest – is that you can use them as a basis for guessing what topics will come up this year, but they will serve more and more important purposes than this. They are the starting point for learning what the examiners – who will often be your teachers – are looking for. You can use past papers to help you learn how your teachers think about their subject and what they give high marks for; you can use them to help you improve your skill at interpreting exam questions and structuring your answers; and you can use them to help you focus your reading and your note-taking over the final weeks before the exam. I deal with all of these in this book.

But there are important precautions to take. Ask your teachers the questions set out in Checklist 2, and make your own comparison of past papers to see if the style has been consistent over the years. If it hasn't been consistent, ask why not: what has changed?

Checklist 2: Past exam papers

Is last year's exam paper a reliable guide to this year's? Will the structure – e.g. the number of questions on the paper and the number to be answered, and the division of the paper into sections – be the same?	As a general rule, exam papers will be set two to three months before you sit the exam, so examiners should be able from that point on to answer these queries.
Is the course a new one?	If so, there naturally won't be any past papers. Ask to be given a sample ('mock') exam paper. This is established practice in at least some places and there is no reason why it should not be so everywhere. Ask if your university has a code of practice that covers this point.
Has the content of the course changed this year? Has it been remodelled in any significant way? Is the course being taught by someone who didn't teach it last year?	Again, ask for sample exam questions.

Box 1

What exactly is an exam question?

Although academics talk about exam papers as comprising a set of questions, requiring answers, in many subjects many of these are not 'direct' questions. That's to say, they aren't 'interrogative sentences': they don't end in a question mark (?). Instead, such 'questions' are in fact instructions: Discuss! Evaluate! and so on. Following customary practice, I use the word 'question' to include both instructions and direct questions. If I'm specifically considering direct questions, I refer to them as such.

What to look for in past exam papers

There are two broad types of exam question: problem questions and essay questions. Problem questions, which supply you with certain data and require you to reason from them to a solution, are found primarily in quantitative subjects and in Law ('Advise X'). Problem questions require you to apply specialized techniques, and these are necessarily beyond the scope of this guide. So here I concentrate on essay questions.

When you look at a past exam paper for the first time, it may leave you unmoved – your state of mind is merely one of curiosity – or it may bring up stronger feelings, ranging from excitement, if it unleashes a flow of adrenaline in you, to panic, if you've had bad experiences with exams in the past. Some people who have had bad experiences put off looking at past exam papers for as long as they can. If you're tempted to do this, try to allow your curiosity to get the better of you, get together with a friend and just take the plunge! It's best got over with, and then you can move on.

The first thing to do with past papers is to cross-check them against the course you are taking. Here's a 'question types' checklist to help you do this:

Checklist 3: Question types

Do you recognize certain questions as 'the question on X' or 'the question on Y'?	You'll find it very helpful to be able to categorize or characterize questions in this way, not least because your teacher/examiner almost certainly does the same.
Can you associate particular questions with particular components of the course?	See whether the exam paper is divided up in the same way as the course is. This is all part of familiarizing yourself, if not actually making friends, with exam papers. If the course is divided up between several teachers, you may be able to identify questions that 'belong' to particular individuals.
Alternatively, do the questions 'cut across' components of the course?	For example, during the year you may have gone through 20 case studies at the rate of one a week, in the process applying to them a total of a dozen or so different theoretical approaches. In contrast to this pattern of work, the exam paper may be divided up not by case studies but by the theoretical approaches, perhaps with a question on each. It's as though the subject is a cake that has been sliced vertically for teaching purposes but horizontally for exam purposes. If so, you certainly need to be forewarned. You also need to know if the exam paper is likely to contain a mixture of types of question, some on particular case studies and some on particular theoretical approaches.

It's worth taking a few minutes to study the language – the actual words – in which exam questions are expressed. This can give you useful clues to how your teachers think: how they conceive of their subject or discipline, what they look for in what they study, how they conceptualize and make sense of it. The questions in the next checklist, Checklist 4, are designed to help you to sensitize yourself to the language of exam papers, and thereby to think yourself into your teachers' mindsets. Check your impressions from this exercise against your recollections of lectures and your lecture notes and handouts, and modify them if necessary. You may be able to refine the above descriptions by identifying particular schools of thought that your teachers belong to.

The more effectively you can think yourself into your teachers' mindsets, the better the idea you will have of the 'style' in which you are expected to answer the questions.

So look at the questions in past exam papers and ask the questions in Checklist 4.

Checklist 4: The language of exam questions

Look out for:	*Expect that:*
Abstract words, such as 'theory', 'perspective', 'concept' and 'paradigm'.	The examiners will be fluent in this language and the relevant literature. To gain high marks you must demonstrate your own fluency in this language and your own command of the literature.
Questions that include the names of and quotations from great writers or theorists on the subject.	The examiners see the subject as defined by writings, theoretical perspectives, debates and critiques, rather than in terms of phenomena in the real world. Again you must demonstrate your command of the literature, and show that you have been able to 'digest' it and apply your own mind to it.
The instruction to 'discuss', to 'comment on', or to 'consider the view that . . .', or the question 'Do you agree?'	The examiners see the subject in terms of themes, whose aspects you should consider, or of debates or arguments conducted inside the academic world,

and will look favourably on answers that cite various and opposing views.

Questions that explicitly or implicitly call for explanation:

- Direct questions that begin with 'Why', 'What', 'Which', 'When', 'How', and variants such as 'To what extent', 'To what degree', 'Under what circumstances', 'In what ways', 'How important was', 'How significant was'.
- The instruction to 'explain' or 'account for' an occurrence (event), situation, etc.
- Words and expressions in direct questions or statements that imply cause and effect: 'because', 'due to', 'linked/related to', 'responsible for', 'caused', 'led to', 'brought about', 'prompted', 'consequences of', 'a product of', 'precipitated', 'made it possible/impossible', 'factors behind/underlying', 'motivated', 'foundations were laid', 'it was no accident that'.

The examiners have a sense – intuitive, if not spelled out and made explicit – of 'how explaining is done' in the subject, and of what constitutes a good or satisfactory explanation. If your teachers have recourse to theories, concepts and authoritative opinion, you must do the same, 'looking out' from the academic world to the real world and giving literature-based answers. But if the subject is taught as a very practical one, an explanation solely in terms of, say, prior events, 'factors', structures, processes or motivations within the real world may be sufficient.

Issue- and action-related words and expressions, of three kinds:

- Those that use the language of issues and actions, e.g. 'issues', 'problems', 'goals', 'objectives', 'priorities', 'outcomes', 'impact', 'costs', 'benefits', 'merits'.
- Those that convey an imperative, notably 'should', 'ought', 'must', 'needs to', 'problem', 'pressure'.

The examiners see their subject in terms of issues ('What should be done about X?') and past, present and future actions. You should do the same, using the same language. Your teachers may well use 'raw', real-world data and literature in a quite eclectic fashion, in which case it should be open to you to follow suit.

- Those that are overtly judgmental, such as 'good/bad', 'fair/unfair', 'a success/a failure', 'right/wrong', 'appropriate/inappropriate'.

Time-related words and expressions, of two kinds:

- Specifying points or periods in time; dates, time spans or frequencies: 'has/have been', 'has/have/will become', 'today', 'currently', 'still', 'rarely', 'sometimes', 'frequently', 'often', 'always'.
- Specifying time-related processes: 'development', 'evolution', sequences and successions of events or situations.

The examiners see their subject in historical terms, even if they are not historians. Again, you should do the same.

Unfair questions

It is by no means unknown for examiners to set questions that are, to put it bluntly, unfair. They are unfair because they confuse candidates. They are worded in such a way that they don't give candidates a clear and comprehensible instruction. Such questions add considerably to the stress of the exam situation, especially for candidates who think that if they cannot understand what is wanted it is their own fault. I imagine that many teachers and departments go to some trouble to ensure that questions are unambiguous and written in clear, grammatical English. Unfortunately this result is not uniformly achieved. Checklist 5 contains a list of types of unfair questions to look out for.

Checklist 5: Unfair questions

Wording	*Source of confusion*
A 'direct' question (one that has a question mark after it) followed by a sentence beginning 'Discuss . . .' or similar. *What role do the media play in relation to gender? Discuss in relation to one type of media product.* (The instruction ought to read: Answer with reference to . . .)	You're getting two conflicting messages. One is telling you to *answer* the question; the other is telling you to *discuss* it. If you realize this, it won't be clear to you which you should do. Many candidates dive into answering the question, but trail away into confusion because they subliminally also get the 'discuss' message.
A statement that isn't in quotation marks, and looks like a statement of fact rather than opinion, followed by a direct question. *There is rapidly growing concern about the sexual rights of children. What should be done to safeguard these rights?* (Are you expected or entitled to ask whether the concern is indeed rapidly growing, and whether it is rapidly growing everywhere?)	Because of the absence of quotation marks, it isn't clear to you whether you are expected or entitled to challenge the statement, or should not challenge it, even if you think it is factually wrong (in whole or in part) or should be qualified.
A statement that isn't in quotation marks, but looks like a statement of opinion, followed by 'Discuss'. *The most promising approach to classifying security risks within an organization involves the use of control mechanisms. Discuss.* (Are you expected or entitled to challenge the opinion that this is 'the most promising approach', or should you merely deal with alternative ways of using control mechanisms, and their consequences?)	Because of the absence of quotation marks, it isn't clear to you whether (a) the statement is indeed offered as a statement of opinion and you are expected or entitled to challenge it, or (b) you should not challenge it, but merely deal with what follows from it.

A double question, i.e. two questions one after the other (as opposed to a question in two parts).
Account for the decline of private rented housing in the UK after 1918. What could and should the Government do to support this sector? (Two separate topics here.)

In effect, you have to think about, plan and write *two* answers in the time allotted for just one.

A quotation followed by a question that doesn't refer to the quotation and would be perfectly comprehensible on its own, if the quotation weren't present.
'I am all the daughters of my father's house, And all the brothers too' (Shakespeare, Twelfth Night*). Compare and contrast two or more representations of sex and gender in literature.* (The 'compare and contrast' instruction can be followed without referring to the quotation. Would it be permissible to do this?)

It isn't clear to you whether or not you are expected to refer to the quotation in your answer.

A question that incorporates a metaphor or colloquial language.
'The cost of social security is the Achilles heel of British social policy.' Discuss. (What is meant by the metaphor 'Achilles heel' in this context?)
Why should we care whether social interactions produce human capital externalities? (The expression 'Why should we care?' is not a rigorous, academic one.)

It isn't clear to you whether you are expected or entitled to answer in similar non-rigorous language, or whether you'll be penalized if you do. And if English isn't your first language, you may not understand a question that employs a metaphor or colloquial language.

A question that incorporates an ambiguous expression, i.e. an expression that could be interpreted in two or more ways.
To what extent is the control of family size the key to economic development in

It isn't clear to you how you are expected to interpret the question. You may waste time puzzling out which of two interpretations is the appropriate one; you may not realize there is more than one way of interpreting the

any country? (Here, 'any country' could mean 'any country in the whole world' or 'any one country of your choice'.)	question and choose the 'wrong' one; or you may realize half-way through writing your answer that there is more than one interpretation. None of these is a good situation to be in.
A question that is over-complicated. *Critically examine why it is necessary to design social policy from a gender perspective.* (Had the question been worded 'Critically examine the claim that it is necessary . . .' it would have been much easier to comprehend and arguably called for the same answer.) *To what extent can it be argued that the European powers failed diplomatically in the aftermath of the break-up of Yugoslavia?* (Had this question been worded 'Assess the assertion that the European powers . . .', again it would have been much easier to comprehend and arguably called for the same answer.)	Over-complication in a question tests not knowledge of the subject but comprehension of English, the ability to identify the status of expressions (especially claims and assertions), and the experience and confidence to divine quickly and accurately what it is that the examiners are looking for.
A question that actually incorporates a mistake, such as a word left out.	This is a rarity, but by no means unknown. It wastes candidates' time, is distracting, and increases stress.

If you find any of these in a past exam paper, challenge your teachers about it at the earliest opportunity. Ask them how the question should be answered, and what you should do if you get a similar question in the paper that you'll be taking. Try to do this early in the year or semester, before the exam papers that you will be taking are set. At the very least do it in a revision session, if your teacher offers one. This ought not require bravery on your part, and perhaps the standard will improve. If a past paper – or, worse, a sequence of past papers – shows several signs of carelessness or inability on the part of examiners to put themselves in the position of a candidate, get your student representatives to ask the department or the university authorities what procedures they have in place to vet and proof-read draft exam papers.

The guessing game: What topics will come up this year?

Guessing what topics will come up in forthcoming exams is entirely a matter for your own skill, judgment and preparedness to take risks, so I can't and won't advise you on it. But there are some questions you could ask to help you take your decisions, and I've listed these in Checklist 6.

Checklist 6: Guessing this year's topics

Are there particular topics that come up year after year?	If so, note the different ways of asking a question about each one, and be prepared for a new variation on an old question.
Is the course kept up to date from year to year?	Might there be a question on a new book or current issue that it would be worth preparing for?
Do past papers appear to have covered the whole of thc course?	Quite likely if you've had 20 classes and there are 20 questions, including *either/ors*, on the paper.
Or do the examiners tend to choose just some of the year's topics for the exam paper?	If so, any selection that you make of topics to revise is inevitably going to be more of a gamble.
Were the lectures given by a number of teachers?	If so, are there signs that exam papers have been compiled by putting together questions contributed by the various lecturers? (Check whether past exam papers are 'compartmentalized' – divided up – in the same way as the course.)
Are papers in this subject divided into parts?	If so, you should already be aware of the basis on which this is done and of the consequent restriction on how narrow your selection of topics can be.
Is there a tendency for two (or more) topics to be covered in a single question or to be bracketed together as an *either/or*?	If so, you must allow for the possibility that some of those you have chosen to revise may be ruled out by this.

Box 2

What examiners are looking for

In my 28 years of experience marking exam papers and sitting on boards of examiners, I have been able to get some sense of how examiners approach marking. While some do have fixed ideas about how exam answers in their subject should be written, so their standpoint is basically critical, the majority I've encountered have an attitude that *appreciates* the merits of answers. Command of the subject matter is of course essential, but they also like to see – and will reward – some or all of the following:

- An answer that is to the point, that actually answers the question.
- A systematic, logical and appropriate structure for your answer.
- Evidence that you have read reasonably widely. If you draw on just one book for an answer – or worse, one book for the whole exam paper – they will not be impressed.
- Signs of independent, critical thinking. Don't be intimidated by this: it comes with familiarity with the subject and from reading and applying your mind to books and articles that take different views of a subject and bring out different aspects of it.
- Evidence of some ability to operate at both high and low levels: to see both the 'big picture' – the overview, the principles, the context – and significant details.
- Evidence of some ability to see connections and to handle a complex subject without oversimplifying it.
- Persuasive advocacy in subjects where you are expected to put forward a point of view and argue for it.
- A dash of originality and imagination. This is often the 'icing on the cake' that marks out a first-class answer.

When it comes to preparing for exams, it is the first two in this list that need particular attention, and in this guide I focus on them in particular. You should of course have been reading and thinking throughout the year or semester, but you should find that formulating model answers helps you a lot in widening your reading and sharpening your thinking.

Part Two

Formulating model answers

Interpreting the question

If you're to do well in exams you *must* have a well-developed technique for interpreting questions. It is a characteristic of poor, off-the-point exam answers that they 'dive' into the subject without any interpretation of the question. Practising on past exam papers, especially if you can get some feedback on your efforts, is an excellent way of learning and developing that technique. You almost certainly won't get the identical questions this year, but that's irrelevant: what you're doing is developing skills that will enable you to interpret and respond to virtually any question that might come up.

Apart from its other benefits, having a good exam technique will help you to write exam answers that are to the point. There is probably not a single university teacher in the UK who doesn't exhort his or her students: 'Answer the question!' You will lose marks if you write an essay in an exam that answers a different question – e.g. a question that you used as an essay topic during the year, or a question that you are substituting for the one on the exam paper – or if you try to write everything you know on the subject, but all too often candidates do exactly that.

Before you can answer the question, you *must* read it carefully and work out (a) what you are expected to put in your answer, and (b) if expectations are unclear, as is often the case, what to put in that will command the examiners' respect. Doing this involves interpreting the question. That's to say, you must pay attention to all the words and work out for yourself what their significance is, individually and collectively.

Checklist 7, 'Interpreting the question', suggests how to do this. Ask yourself the questions in the left-hand column. This will do four things for you: (a) It will help you to comprehend the intricacies of the question; (b) it will help you to deal coolly with any ambiguities you come across rather than be rattled by them; (c) it will help to keep you focused on the question while writing your answer; and (d) it will generate worthwhile points to make under the heading of 'Interpretation' in the introduction to your answer. (See 'Drawing up a plan', pages 45-49.) Even if the examiners' expectations aren't made clear in the question's instructions, you have a systematic and organized approach to interpreting the question for which they can't avoid giving you credit.

Checklist 7: Interpreting the question

Ask yourself . . .	*Points to make under 'interpretation'*
Are there words or expressions in the question which different writers use in different ways, i.e. to which they attribute different meanings? *'Globalization is of undoubted benefit to the world's poor.' Discuss.* 'Globalization' is currently a prime example of a word to which different authors attribute different meanings.	Always show that you are aware of these different meanings. It could be appropriate for you to write something about the differences between them. Don't merely say 'A defines . . .' and proceed to use that definition without considering others. Make the point that different writers mean different things by the same word. And it's better practice to think in terms of meanings rather than definitions.

Are there non-specialized words or expressions in the question that can have more than one sense or meaning? *Comment on the view that it is the function of the prime minister to take the lead in the formation of the Government's policy.* The word 'function', like 'role', can be used in either a descriptive sense ('The prime minister does . . .') or a normative sense ('The prime minister ought to . . .').	If the question does not make it clear which sense or meaning is intended, you should point out that more than one is possible. If you are going to adopt one rather than the other, make it clear that you are making a conscious choice.
Does the question incorporate a claim, assertion or opinion? (Pay particular attention to over-complicated questions.) *Critically examine why it is necessary to design social policy from a gender perspective?* (Here the claim is that it *is* necessary to design social policy from this perspective.) *To what extent can it be argued that the European powers failed diplomatically in the aftermath of the break-up of Yugoslavia?* (Here the assertion, 'sign-posted' by the word 'argued', is that the European powers *did* fail diplomatically.)	If the claim, assertion or opinion is not immediately apparent, it is really important to identify it and to show the examiners that you have done so.
Does the question incorporate a metaphor or colloquial language? *'The cost of social security is the Achilles heel of British social policy.' Discuss.* ('Achilles heel' is a metaphor, not a rigorous academic term. Translate it as 'vulnerability or weakness that could lead to collapse or failure'.) *Why should we care whether social*	Metaphors and colloquial language need to be translated into rigorous language if you are to apply reasoning in answering the question.* Sometimes you can gain clarity by asking: 'How would I recognize X if I saw it?' or the methodology question: 'How can I tell?' See the section on 'Methodology', below.

* When you encounter this kind of difficulty ask your teacher for help. If English isn't your first language, you may find it helpful to consult a fellow student who is a native English speaker. In some fields, the language of exam questions can be a rather specialized one, and it is important that you master it.

interactions produce human capital externalities? ('Why should we care?' is colloquial language, not a rigorous academic expression. This question seems to require a discussion of the impact of such externalities (or their absence) on people, and a judgment as to whether these are beneficial or harmful.)

Is part of the question expressed as if it is an incontrovertible statement of fact? If so, is that statement consistent with evidence? Or is it essentially an assumption or a subjective view? *Neighbourhoods form the basic building blocks of social provision and social cohesion. Outline a policy for addressing social problems in run-down urban areas.* (You should feel able to query the first sentence in this question.) *Modernism represents a conscious desire to transgress established categories. To what extent is a striving for novelty evident in American literary modernism?* (Again, you should feel able to query the first sentence in this question.)

You should query all such statements and assure yourself as to their status (i.e. their degree of accuracy/objectivity/subjectivity). If you know that it will be acceptable, state any reservations that you have about them.

Does the question incorporate a generalization of some kind? *'Cities in the South are unhealthy, crime-ridden and chaotic, and should be remodelled on Western principles of urban design.' Discuss.* (Do *all* three adjectives apply to *all* cities in 'the South'?)

You should query all such generalizations.

Methodology

Methodology? What's that? In the context of examinations, your 'methodology' is your way of answering the question: your 'system of methods'.

If you have ever written an essay, you must have employed a methodology, whether you were aware of it or not. You can't *not* have done so. If you weren't aware of it, ask yourself: *how* did I construct that essay? At the very least the answer you give yourself will be along on the lines 'First I looked at X. Then I looked at Y . . .'. Looking at one thing then looking at another – or talking about one thing then talking about another – is about as primitive a methodology as you can find. A 'points for, points against' methodology is not much better. You will need to 'raise your game' if you are to get good exam results.

The challenge, then, is to equip yourself with an explicit, conscious methodology. That is the subject of this section. It is helpful to distinguish between (a) questions that comprise a statement (which should be in quotation marks) plus an instruction (describe, discuss, etc.), and (b) direct, interrogative questions, and to deal with them separately.

First, though, permit me to offer you a wonderfully simple generic question that cuts through many difficulties like a scalpel:

How can I tell?

If you have a statement to deal with, put it this way. Ask yourself: 'How can I tell ... whether this statement is true?' For 'true' you can substitute 'accurate', 'valid', 'supported by evidence', 'a logical inference from the facts', 'based on well-founded suppositions'. The answer that you give to the 'How can I tell?' question is your first shot at making your methodology explicit.

And if you have a direct question to answer, put it like this: 'How can I tell ... what the answer to the question is?' You can rephrase this as: 'What do I have to do to find the answer?' Once again, what you say in response is your first shot at making your methodology explicit.

Statement plus instruction

On the face of it, every instruction accompanying a statement tells you what methodology you should use. On closer inspection, however, it is often very difficult to discern from the instruction exactly what it is that you are expected to do. If you are instructed to *describe* something, that could mean: (a) list the significant characteristics of the subject (in which case you will have to decide which characteristics to regard as significant ones); *or* (b) say in addition *why* you consider these characteristics to be significant; *or* (c) say furthermore how these characteristics are interconnected, e.g. how if one is present others will be. But any of these, especially (b) and (c), could involve you in spending the whole 45 minutes or hour on writing your description.

So how should you proceed? I suggest that you ask yourself: 'How can I tell what the significant characteristics of the subject are, and how much detail to go into?' Almost certainly, you will get useful clues not from the instruction 'describe' but from your interpretation of the remainder of the exam question. To take a simple example, if the remainder of the question is quite complex it is perfectly apparent that you should spend only a little time – and thus only a few words – on your description.

If you are instructed to *analyse* something, that could mean: (a) describe in detail; *or* (b) break down into component parts; *or* (c) show how causes combine to bring about certain effects. You will get clues as to which approach is appropriate from looking at the 'something', not from worrying over what is meant by 'analyse'.

If you are instructed to *compare and contrast*, that could mean: (a) list similarities and differences; *or* (b) formulate and apply criteria that can be used for comparison; *or* (c) in addition, say how the similarities and differences come about. Once again, clues as to how you should proceed will be found in the nature of the things to be compared and contrasted rather than in the instruction.

And if you are instructed to *explain* something, that could mean: (a) say clearly what is meant by . . .; *or* (b) recount how it came about; *or* (c) show how causes combine to bring about certain effects; *or* (d) give reasons why someone behaved in the way they did. Yet again, clues as to how you should proceed will be found in the nature of the 'something' rather than in the instruction 'explain'.

As for 'discuss', 'discuss critically', 'comment on the view that . . .' and 'do you agree?', these are all highly vague and unspecific instructions. What you must do, accordingly, is take your cue from your interpretation of the statement in the question.

Do not assume that the examiners are much clearer than you are about their instructions, and that there are right answers to the non-quantitative questions that they set. They may vary instructions from question to question simply for the sake of variety. And they may set questions to see what you make of them, or to give you the opportunity to demonstrate the breadth of your reading, the depth of your understanding, and/or your ability to approach questions in a systematic and structured way.

Direct questions

With a direct, interrogative, question, the (implicit) instruction is to answer it. But even direct questions require to be interpreted, and once you have done this you are still left asking: 'How can I tell what the answer is?' Here again, as with statements plus instructions, you have to look to the wording of the question to come up with your methodology.

So let's look at the wording of both kinds of questions. In Checklist 8, Methodology, I offer some suggestions for identifying what it is that the question is inviting you to do.

Checklist 8: Methodology

Ask yourself . . .	*Implications for methodology*
Does the question invite comparisons? *Compare and contrast . . .* *'Culture is the most important factor in . . .' Discuss.* *To what extent . . .?*	If you are explicitly asked to 'compare and contrast', you will usually gain credit for saying what criteria you are using and what aspects you are going to contrast. This applies whatever it is that you are comparing/contrasting. In general, if you do no more than list similarities and differences you will not get a particularly good mark. Note that the instruction to compare and contrast may be *implicit*. Look out for statements such as 'A is the most significant/important factor in . . .', and questions beginning 'To what extent is A . . .?' Always read these as meaning 'A rather than B – or C, D, E etc.' The words 'major', 'minor', 'more' and 'most' have a similar comparative connotation, as do 'so much' and similar expressions.
Does the question invite you to comment on a theory, model, paradigm or hypothesis? *How useful is X's theory of . . .?* *Which theoretical perspectives do you feel contribute most to contemporary debates on . . .?* *Explore the differences between the interpretative paradigm and the functionalist paradigm in relation to . . .'* *Critically discuss Y's concept of . . .'*	Be prepared to outline the attributes of the theory, say, and to test it. (1) Attributes. These include concepts, underlying assumptions (premises, postulates), variables, and relationships between variables. You will need to know what is meant by the various words used (so be prepared to supply translations of them into more usual language if necessary). (2) Tests. These include: 'fit with the

'Z's conceptual distinction . . . provides a valuable tool for . . .' Discuss.

facts', internal logical consistency, consistency with other theories, usefulness as a basis for making predictions or formulating proposals for action. Most fundamentally, ask: 'What does this theory reveal? What does it help us to understand? In what ways does it go beyond providing a rarefied language for describing things that are already well known?'

Does the question invite you to explain an effect, which implies elucidating a causal (cause-and-effect) relationship? For example:

- Direct questions, such as
  Why does . . .?
  To what extent . . .?
  Under what circumstances . . .?
  How significant was . . .?
  What factors are driving change in . . .?
- Instructions, such as
  Explain . . .
  Account for . . .
- Words and expressions in direct questions or statements that imply cause and effect. For example
  'A was responsible for . . .'
  'B was a product of . . .'
  'C laid the foundation for . . .'
  'It was no accident that . . .'

Do your best to 'tease out', make explicit, the causal connection. You should have noticed how your teachers explain effects, and what they regard as a good or satisfactory explanation. If they have never made these clear to you, bear in mind that hardly any event or situation has a single 'cause', and try to distinguish some or all of the following:

- Pre-existing conditions (e.g. political, economic, cultural, social, demographic, military)
- 'Triggering' events
- 'Promoting' factors: motivations, goals, objectives
- 'Enabling' factors: resources, opportunities
- Mechanisms, processes (e.g. diplomatic, political, bureaucratic, demographic, economic; decision-making; growth, change)
- Structures (e.g. power structures, legislative frameworks, markets, social structures).

Use counterfactual (what if?) reasoning if your teachers do, asking – for example –

not just 'Why did X happen?' but 'Why did X rather than Y happen?'

Does the question invite you to comment on or discuss someone's claim, assertion, opinion or argument? For example:
Comment on the view that . . .
Do you agree?
'The only way to . . . is by . . .' Discuss.

Treat this claim, say, as requiring to be tested or challenged.

- Testing against evidence. You should be clear as to whether the test should be one of *consistency* with empirical evidence or the weaker one of *plausibility*, appealing essentially to intuition (albeit the intuition of experts). You can test the assertion, say, against both the author's evidence and evidence from other sources.
- Testing for logic. You can scrutinize the reasoning behind an assertion etc. for internal inconsistencies, omissions, selective use of evidence, and bias. You can check whether the conclusions that someone has drawn from their study do actually follow from the data they obtained rather than from the assumptions they made at the outset.
- Challenging. Has another writer (or your teacher) put forward a contradictory claim, assertion, opinion or argument? Think about how you can tell who deserves your support.

Does the question use issue- and action-related words and expressions? For example:
Assess the impact of . . .
What were the objectives of . . . and to what extent were they met?
What problems does X pose for . . .?

Look for the imperative: why does anything at all need to be done? In the case of references to 'problems', always ask for whom 'it' is a problem. Always consider alternative courses of action, and constraints (limitations) on action, and try to trace the possible impact on

What are the advantages and disadvantages of X for . . .? *Why is the Government under pressure to do X, and what should its response be?* *'Policy X was a disaster.' Discuss.*	or outcome for all individuals and groups who might be affected. Sometimes you will need to put yourself in the position of a decision-maker or manager; sometimes in the position of an objective observer. You may be asked to put forward your own value judgment as to the merits of a proposed course of action, but your marks are more likely to depend on how well you trace impact/outcome than on the values you bring to bear. It may well be permissible to use whatever 'raw', real-world data and literature you have available, so long as it is relevant.
Does the question invite you to conduct a debate?	Be prepared to list the main points at issue and deal with them in turn. You may want to do this by considering the relevant 'pros and cons'. Be wary when introducing qualifications, i.e. whenever you feel the urge to say 'it depends'. These can lead you off your main 'track'.
Is there a 'hidden' second question?	With a question like ' "B is the consequence of A." Discuss.', be aware of the implied 'hidden' question: 'Is B the consequence of other factors, or of the conjunction of A and other factors?' Be prepared to discuss that possibility.

Materials

In the previous section I showed how to work out from the wording of a question the methodology that you need in order to answer it. Methodologies have to be *applied*. And what they are applied to, always, is *materials*. Even when writing an essay 'off the top of your head', you must be using *some* materials in writing your answer. These might take the form of 'raw' data, research reports, ideas that you've found in the literature, or any of the other items listed in the left-hand column of Checklist 9.

Checklist 9: Materials

Kinds of material	*What to do with them or about them*
'Raw' material, empirical evidence, information, data	Ask yourself what is actually known about the subject. Be prepared to cite the relevant evidence or 'facts', and to say what data sources you have used and what their limitations are.
Case studies and other research reports, and authors' inferences from them	Say why you have chosen these particular ones. Very often, to keep your answer brief, you will have to make a 'trade-off between breadth and depth', e.g. between several case studies treated somewhat shallowly (salient features only) or a select few treated in more detail.
Classical texts; narrative and descriptive material	It's unlikely that you will get high marks for reproducing passages from these. Marks are usually awarded for comprehending texts and appreciating their significance, not for memorizing them. Pick out the relevant points.
Original works written for an academic audience: works of theory, criticism or commentary	You should 'gut' these works to extract their significant points. It could be worth while memorizing, or being able to paraphrase, a few sentences that summarize these points.
Journal articles, which may report on specific pieces of work, review a field of study, or constitute contributions to a debate	Usually useful for brief, specific points only.
Textbooks, secondary sources	May give an overview, but should only be used if there is no alternative. Try not to write like a textbook yourself.
Specialized material, such as law reports and statutes; reference works	You should have learned during the year how you are expected to make use of

	these. Check beforehand if you are able to take any of these into the examination or if copies will be supplied. It is crucial that you are able to find your way around them speedily during the exam.
Advocacy, polemic or argument, coming from a particular point of view	You will usually be expected to analyse and discuss such material impartially, not to support or attack it in the same style. In particular, avoid asking rhetorical questions.
Newspapers, magazine articles, pictorial images, television and radio transcripts, and other ephemera	Distinguish between reportage and opinion. Treat critically: watch out for selectivity and bias in both.

Drawing up a plan

Once you are clear about your methodology and the materials that you are going to use, it's time to draw up a plan, the outline of the exam answer you are going to write. Checklist 10 offers a general model for doing this. I hope you will find it a useful model to follow, but because it is a general model it is important that you adapt it to your particular needs.

In effect, Checklist 10 takes you through an exercise in drawing up a plan. I strongly suggest that you do the exercise in two stages. First of all, draw up your plan 'in rough', as a list of bullet points or headings. Then go over it again putting in more detail. The great benefit of doing it in this way is that once you have a picture in your mind of the whole answer, *especially your conclusions*, you will have a better sense of 'where your answer is going', and thus of what to include and what to leave out.

Checklist 10: Points to cover in drawing up a plan

INTRODUCTION
(This can be one or two paragraphs, depending on how much you have to say.)

- Context/background. You may like to begin your introduction with a sentence outlining the context or setting the background. If you're sure it would be relevant and appropriate (if it's something that your teachers do), you could use a quotation here.
- Interpretation. Referring back to Checklist 6, say how you are interpreting problematic terms or colloquial language. Identify ambiguities, assumptions, etc., and say how you will deal with them. Draw attention to any hidden questions.
- Methodology. Then continue: 'In this essay I shall . . .' (or 'This essay will . . .' if your teachers don't like essays written in the first person) and outline the particular methods you will be using. This will usually require no more than a sentence or two, but if you think there are any difficulties to do with your methodology it will probably be worth saying what these are and how you have dealt with them.
- Materials. Then say very briefly, referring back to Checklist 8, what materials you will be using, and why. If you have had to be selective, say how you have made your selection.
- Outline of following sections. End your introduction by saying very briefly what the following sections of your essay will contain. If your teachers like you to say at the outset what your conclusion will be, a sentence beginning 'It will be

concluded/shown/argued that . . .'
should satisfy them.

FINDINGS, REASONING/ANALYSIS and RESULTS

'Findings' will be taken directly from your material. 'Reasoning' and 'analysis' are what you do when you apply your methodology to your material. 'Results' are what you get from doing this; they are what you show or demonstrate.

DISCUSSION

If your results fall into a number of parts, or 'strands', your discussion will usually consider them together. It could cover:

- The implications of your results. These might include (a) value judgments that you have reached (e.g. of merits and demerits); (b) comments that you have on theories, ideas etc. that you encountered in the literature; (c) the significance of your results, e.g. for future developments in the field; for research; for the policies and practices of government bodies, businesses etc. If you have been asked to discuss a statement, you will need to set out the conditions under which it holds ('is true'), or the qualifications or limitations that you feel must be attached to it ('it depends').
- The validity of your results. What confidence do you have in them? Are they universally valid? How far can one safely generalize from them?
- The process: methodology issues. If you encounter limitations or other problems in applying your methods to your material, don't gloss over them: say what they were and outline their implications for the confidence you have in your results.

CONCLUSIONS	The briefest possible summary of your discussion. This is just to draw threads together, for the reader's benefit. Include the salient points only. You won't earn any marks for repeating yourself. 'Revisit' your starting point. Summarize in one or two sentences your answer to the exam question set or the view you have formed on the statement you were asked to discuss.

Important note: You can use the headings 'Introduction', 'Discussion' and 'Conclusions' as headings in your essay. But it may be best not to use 'Findings', 'Reasoning', 'Analysis' or 'Results' as headings. Instead use headings appropriate to your subject, methodology and materials. For example, if you are writing about African cities your headings might be 'Lagos', 'Accra', 'Nairobi'. If you are writing about American poets your headings might be 'Ezra Pound', 'Langston Hughes' and 'e.e. cummings'. However, if you are presenting factual information and then analysing it, it would be appropriate to have 'Salient features' (say) followed by 'Analysis'.

Incidentally, everyone finds that plans like these go through several versions before the final one is reached. Do not aim for perfection first time: something rough and ready will be adequate to get you started. Ideas for improving it will occur to you as you go along. But as you become more and more practised at formulating model answers you will find that it takes fewer and fewer versions before you arrive at one that is good and serviceable.

A final thought on the benefits of drawing up plans and formulating model answers. The more experience I have of seeing students do this, the more convinced I have become of its value not only as an aid to exam preparation but also as an aid to *learning*. Think of it like this. You have a certain volume of knowledge to master, spread over a wide area and going into some depth. In tackling a limited number of questions you are covering only patches of this area, but you are drilling 'boreholes' into that volume of knowledge, so you are exploring those patches in some depth. As you drill more boreholes you are building up your three-dimensional picture of the volume. You really don't need to excavate the whole area (and in any case usually it simply isn't feasible to spread your efforts so widely): strategically placed boreholes will give you what you need. In particular, just like a geologist, from your boreholes you are getting a clear idea of the subject's structure: the layers of knowledge, the theoretical underpinnings, etc. Equally important, you are also developing your 'borehole drilling' technique.

An alternative approach: the 'question string'

This approach to structuring exam answers involves reformulating the question in the form of a 'string' of questions. The simplest way of illustrating this is with an example.

Take the hypothetical exam question: 'Anti-poverty policies can never succeed.' Discuss.

(Note that exam questions as short as this always require you to create your own structure, unlike long ones, which offer you some help.)

Your 'question string' might look like this:

- What is meant by 'poverty'?
- What is meant by an 'anti-poverty policy'?
- What criteria of success can I use (e.g. whether outcomes match intentions)?

- Do I want to restrict my answer geographically (to a locality, region, country or continent)?
- What case studies can I use?
- What information do I have about the form that anti-poverty policies take or have taken (statements of intention/legislation/allocation of resources etc.)?
- What were the actual intentions of the 'policy makers'?
- How were the policies implemented?
- What were the outcomes?
- Did the outcomes match the intentions?
- Has there been more success in some cases than others?
- How can variations be explained (lack of resources/lack of political will/local factors affecting implementation, etc.)?
- Which of these can be characterized as 'impediments to success'?
- Under what circumstances/conditions are these impediments less likely to occur/more likely to be easily overcome?
- What are the policy implications of my findings?

As you can see, the exam question has been 'translated' into 15 'sub-questions'. Answer these in turn, and there's your answer to the original question. Once you have identified your sub-questions, your exam answer almost writes itself!

You can also use your list of questions to put together a neat little introduction, perhaps on the following lines:

> A number of Western governments have adopted domestic anti-poverty policies, and – in conjunction with certain international bodies – policies aimed at relieving poverty in so-called Third World countries. In this essay I shall first consider the problematic terms in the proposition that 'Anti-poverty policies can never succeed.' I shall then examine some examples of anti-poverty policies drawn from different parts of the world, paying attention to the intentions behind them, the measures employed, and the outcomes achieved. I shall show that in some/many/most cases, outcomes fell short of publicized intentions. I shall then identify and discuss the factors that contributed to

these shortfalls, and set out the implications of my findings for future anti-poverty policies.

If, while you're revising, after drawing up your list of sub-questions you realize there are some sub-questions that you can't answer, be aware that you have done something extremely useful: you have identified a gap in your knowledge. You can go to your books, photocopies, lecture notes etc. looking for the specific material you need.

A couple of don'ts. Don't forget to mention the authors whose work you are referring to (e.g. Smith 1992), and in an exam don't use the questions themselves as subheadings (this could make the exam question look too easy, and in any case 15 is too many subheadings: six or so would be about right).

Choose your introduction

The introduction to an essay is its 'launching pad'. Get the introduction right, and you have got off to a good start. It is a reader-friendly thing to do, because it provides 'signposts' to the content of your answer (don't forget that the examiner will have dozens or even hundreds of answers to read) and it helps you to do yourself justice. In composing your introduction you'll be sorting your ideas out, and if it's done reasonably well the reader will immediately gain the impression that this is a systematic, organized piece of work. An exam answer that just 'dives in' to the subject is headed for a low mark.

So what should you do? If you've drawn up a plan on the lines discussed in earlier sections, you'll have an introduction divided into five parts: Context/background; Interpretation; Methodology; Materials; Outline of following sections. In many cases all these parts will be essential, but sometimes you won't consider it necessary to include all of them – you might feel that it's not necessary to include anything on context/background, or that the question is so straightforward that no interpretation is necessary – and sometimes you might wish to change the order, especially if your teacher has made it very clear what he or she wants to see. For example, some like to read in an introduction 'This essay will argue that . . .'. Others prefer to read instead 'In this essay I shall investigate . . .'.

Accordingly, if you've drawn up a five-part introduction on the lines I've suggested, take a fresh look at it. It should be apparent to you that you could have written it – and in particular, started it – in a number of different ways.

Here are a number of possible openings:

- 'In this essay I will draw on evidence provided by two (three, four) case studies to test the proposition that . . .'
- 'To find an explanation for this phenomenon it is necessary to examine a number of factors and how they interacted . . .'
- 'In order to understand A's behaviour it is necessary to explore his motivation, the resources available to him, and the opportunity open to him to deploy those resources . . .'
- 'B's theory of . . . has recently been criticized by C, D and E. In order to assess the validity of these criticisms . . .'
- 'In order to gauge the effect of . . . on . . ., it is necessary to investigate the part that it plays in the process of . . .'
- 'Different writers define . . . in different ways. For the purpose of this essay I shall use F's definition, because it enables a distinction to be drawn between . . .'
- ' ". . ." is not a technical or scientific term but a colloquial one. For the purpose of this essay I shall take it to mean . . .'
- 'Whether X was beneficial or not is a value judgment. In this essay I shall consider its impact on the different groups affected by it and then make my personal judgment as to whether the benefits for some outweighed the costs borne by others . . .'
- 'There is a large and varied literature on . . . Writers approach the subject from a wide range of perspectives. For example, . . .'

- 'The issue of whether governments should do Y has arisen in the past n years. G argues that . . .'
- 'The origins of Z can be traced to . . .'

Which of these would your teachers favour? In effect, every undergraduate or Master's student has several little research projects to carry out, to find the answer to this question for each subject studied.

One approach you can use is this. Go back to your essay plan, and write four different introductions to the essay: use four of the above models, or any others that occur to you. Then adapt your essay plan to produce four versions, one to go with each introduction.

Then show the four essay plans plus introductions to your teacher and ask which one he or she considers most appropriate, and why.

And when you get an answer, follow it up by asking if there are any apparent omissions or errors or traps that you need to be wary of. If necessary, ask if you can submit a revised version for comments. Take full advantage of office hours and revision classes. And if your fellow students adopt the same strategy, compare notes with them.

Warning! You may be tempted to start your answer with a quotation that you have memorized. By all means try out this approach on your teacher too. But be aware that it is a very, very risky thing to do, because it leads you to focus on the quotation rather than the question, and as a result you are highly likely to fail to consider the question fully and answer it properly. My advice is: don't do it, unless you are 100 per cent certain that it is completely appropriate to the question!

Argument or chain of reasoning?

There are some teachers who see their subject in terms of *arguments*. They use the words 'argue' and 'argument' a great deal: 'In this lecture I shall argue that . . .', 'So-and-so argues that . . .', 'My argument is . . .'.

Sadly, despite repeatedly enquiring, I have hardly ever met a student who has been told by a teacher 'This is how academics in my subject construct an argument', or 'This is how to do arguing.' But I *have* met many students who have started writing an essay with the words 'In this essay I shall argue that . . .' and then found themselves completely at a loss as to how to structure the remainder of the essay.

I think the problem is this. Students who have been told by their teacher 'I want to see a clear argument' and then been given direct questions ('Why did . . .?') have a problem because *an argument is not an answer to a question.*

Answering a direct question entails setting out a chain of reasoning leading from the question at the beginning to the answer at the end. You work your way – applying your methodology to your materials – via a chain of reasoning from Q to A. But putting forward an argument entails stating your conclusion, your A, at the very beginning, and then making a series of points to back it up. So when answering a direct question you reach your conclusion at the end; when putting forward an argument you're effectively stating your conclusion at the beginning. It's no wonder that you get confused when you try to do both things at once.

Furthermore, if you start off by stating your conclusion you may be tempted to concentrate on evidence that supports your conclusion and to ignore evidence that would not support it. It's much better, in my view, to express yourself neutrally, e.g. 'In this essay I shall examine/investigate whether . . .'.

Now, it may be that when your teachers say they want to see a 'clear' or a 'strong' argument they are using the word 'argument' in the sense of advocacy: to argue is to advocate, to make a case, to try to persuade someone of the rightness of your point of view. So a good argument is one is that is 'persuasive' or even merely 'plausible'. If you are absolutely certain that this kind of argument is indeed what's called for, then it should be safe to begin an exam answer with the words 'In this essay I shall argue . . .' and to go on to supply a list of points to back it up.

But if it has been dinned into you by your teachers that you have to supply an argument and then in an exam you are asked a direct question, I suggest that you follow the structure for an introduction shown in Checklist 10 and end the outline of the following sections with the words 'It will be shown/concluded that . . .'. Even the most argumentative academic will be unable to fault that.

Writing exam answers: some more suggestions

When deciding which questions to answer, don't be put off by long questions. Invariably they are offering you a structure, a 'handle' on the question. The shorter the question, the more you have to make up a structure for yourself.

Beware the seductiveness of history (except in history exams, of course). Do not spend time on a historical introduction unless the question specifically asks for it or it is directly relevant.

Be even-handed. Where there are two sides to a question, show that you are aware of both of them, even if you come down firmly on one side rather than the other. You are not marked on your political views, but don't allow a bias to get in the way of a reasoned analysis, or a critique to become a polemic.

At the risk of repeating myself: *do* direct your answer to the question. In particular, be careful in your use of 'prepared answers'.

When you see a question on topic X, this is *not* an invitation to you to reproduce an essay that you once wrote on X and subsequently memorized. (In general, you don't get marks for memorizing.) Your answer *must* be an answer to the question put, not to some other question.

Similarly, a question on X is *not* an invitation to you to write everything you know about X.

Limit the amount of description in your answers. Description in itself is not very interesting to examiners. They will want to assure themselves that you possess the necessary factual material, but they are more interested in what you do with it.

Do not, in the course of your answer, ask rhetorical questions. In an examination situation, the protocol is that the examiners ask the questions; you supply answers.

Referencing. You are not expected to be as punctilious in referencing exam answers as you are in assessed essays and other work written in your own time. But go beyond mere name-dropping if you can. Examiners will appreciate 'Smith (1992)', 'Jones, in her book . . .', 'Smith and Jones, in their recent paper in . . .'. Try to get the titles of books and journals right, and underline them in your answers.

Be wary of speculating. There are no marks to be gained for guessing about the future. You might want to extrapolate current trends, or argue from past experience, but usually these are the kind of things to be tacked on as a post-script: they shouldn't form the main part of an answer unless you are absolutely certain that the examiners will reward them.

Remember that your answers don't have to be exhaustive. Some questions are so broad that a dissertation or even a book could be written on them. You will probably have to be selective in the material that you use, but make it clear to the examiners that you are doing so deliberately, not through a lack of material. (Showing examiners how much you know without actually spelling it out in detail is one of the skills associated with doing well in this kind of examination.)

Even if your teachers have no objection to your writing 'I think . . .', it may be best to avoid using that expression and others like it. And avoid 'obviously'. If something really is obvious, you don't need to say that it is. (So using 'obviously' will suggest to the suspicious reader that you don't actually have evidence to support your contention.) The main objection to these terms is that if you get into the habit of using them it will distract you from paying sufficient attention to the evidence. When tempted to say 'I think', always ask yourself 'Do I have evidence for this thought?' Of course, any conclusion that you come to is your personal conclusion, reflecting your personal judgment of the evidence, and there is no intellectual objection to your writing 'In the light of this, I conclude that . . .'.

Do not attribute human characteristics to mental constructs. For example, do not refer to 'the purpose of cost-benefit analysis': it is *people* (in this case the advocates or proponents of cost-benefit analysis) who have a purpose. Likewise it is people (critics or opponents) who will be arguing that a theory or technique does not, when acted on, have the outcomes claimed for it, e.g. because it is not applied correctly or because the underlying assumptions or reasoning are invalid.

Likewise, do not use the words 'reason' or 'means' in situations where reasoning or meaning are not involved (e.g. do not refer to 'the reason why the earth orbits round the sun' or 'global warming means that sea levels will rise').

In the interests of user-friendliness, I have written this book using the informal language of spoken English as much as possible – 'bits' and 'a lot', for example. There are two dangers that you may encounter if you do this in academic writing: it may lead you to be imprecise and it may give the impression that you are sloppy and non-rigorous, or even journalistic – a term of abuse in many academic circles – in your thinking.

I suggest, therefore, that in exam answers (and in all essays that you write) you avoid the following words and expressions (possible alternatives are given in brackets):

- 'it's' (it is) (avoid *all* such contractions)
- 'bits' (parts)
- 'things' (units, elements, factors)
- 'a lot' or 'a load' (a significant amount, a sizeable quantity, considerable numbers)
- 'like' (similar to, such as)
- 'get' (obtain, receive, become)
- 'as well as' (in addition to)
- 'How come . . .?' (What caused, what brought about . . .?)

The rule is: avoid 'chatty' language!

Questions for examiners

It will be helpful to you to know not only what examiners give credit for but also what they might possibly penalize you for. So you should also feel able to ask your teachers these questions:

- Is it acceptable for me to write in the first person (e.g. 'In this essay I shall show . . .' or 'In my judgment, . . .')? Or do you prefer impersonal forms, such as 'This essay will show . . .' or 'One concludes that . . .'?
- Do you prefer essays to be written in the active voice (e.g. 'Germany invaded Poland') rather than the passive voice ('Poland was invaded by Germany')?
- Is it acceptable to use headings and subheadings in my essays? (Some teachers feel that these interfere with the 'flow' of the prose.)

- Is it acceptable to make use of case studies or other materials that weren't on the reading list but I found for myself?
- Will I be penalized for grammatical or spelling mistakes or for using American spellings for words?
- Will I be penalized if I express views that disagree with yours?
- What does an examination answer book look like? (A silly question? Don't under-estimate the ability of higher education institutions to confuse students at critical moments!)

Don't be diffident about asking your teachers questions. Think of academics as puzzles for you to solve. And of one of the purposes of students as being to make academics think!

Box 3

If you have a disability

If you have a physical disability or a recognized condition such as dyslexia that causes you problems with reading and/or writing, you may be entitled to have special exam arrangements made for you, such as being given extra time or allowed to sit the exam in a room in the student health centre. If you think you qualify for such arrangements, it is essential that you apply for them in good time. Do so at the earliest possible opportunity, to allow time for consideration of your case and the carrying out of any assessment of your needs that may be thought necessary. Even before this, find out what the procedure is for applying, and read whatever regulations have been published on the subject of exams and special needs. Always do your homework!

Part Three

In the run up to exams

Revising effectively

Once you're in the run-up to exams, your work has to be very focused. You simply don't have time to sit down and read books and articles from beginning to end.

You may think of revising, or reviewing, as a matter of cramming into your head as much stuff as possible. Don't! If you've been keeping up reasonably well with your work during the year you've already absorbed a considerable amount of knowledge, ideas, approaches, techniques and so on, almost certainly more than you realize. It's up there on the shelves of your subconscious mind. The challenge is how to gain access to all this material – how to retrieve it – and let it out in an orderly fashion on to the pages of your answer book.

So don't spend precious time writing out model exam answers in full or plodding painstakingly through books and articles and lecture notes, highlighting and underlining and making copious notes. Instead, use this time to extract, from your store of notes and other resources already available to you, material that is directly relevant to the topics that you are preparing for. Your store is there for you to use, to interrogate, to ask questions of. Your task is to locate the bits you want, to reach up to the shelves and lift them down into your conscious mind. Then you have to *review* your materials, to cross-check the notes you've made during the year against your sources, and to find any extra material that you need to extend your range or complete a picture. Your brain will enjoy doing this detective work much more than trying to soak up stuff (an activity guaranteed to put you to sleep), and as a result you'll have no difficulty in remembering what you did.

Reviewing and cross-checking may sound rather basic and rudimentary, but it's an important part of integrating the work that you've done during the semester or year. You've been 'drip-fed' the subject week by week: in the run-up to exams, after teaching has finished, you have the chance not only to revise but also to pull everything together into an integrated whole. You can get an overview of the subject, see how everything fits together, notice the underlying harmony.

If you know that past exam papers are going to be a reasonably reliable guide to this year's, dig out those past exam papers and find the questions on the topics you're concentrating on. Note the different ways that questions on that topic can be put, and invent – visualize, 'brainstorm' – some new ones. If past exam papers are *not* going to be a reasonably reliable guide to this year's, then it's particularly important to invent new questions. Use topics that have been covered in lectures and that have been set for seminars, classes or tutorials. Listen carefully for clues you may be given in revision sessions held by your teachers. By all means get together with like-minded fellow students and pool your thoughts. Again, note the different ways that questions on these topic can be put.

Now, take these potential exam questions and brainstorm an essay plan – a list of headings and subheadings, or bullet points if you prefer – for each one. Do it quickly. It only needs to be a rough plan at this stage: ideas for improving it will come into your head unbidden. It's an enormously useful thing to do, for three reasons:

- First, practice at drawing up essay plans will help you in the exam itself, because it will give you an overview of the topic and a logical step-by-step process to follow in writing your answer. As I said early on, it's most people's experience that writing is a twofold activity: there's 'writing as thinking' and 'writing as assembly job'. If you can separate these two activities – first do the thinking as you produce a logical sequence of headings, then slot in a paragraph under each heading – you'll be working very efficiently. Furthermore, if you're writing to a plan you can see at a glance where you've got to, which is exceedingly helpful in tailoring your writing to the time available.
- Second, if your teachers are available and willing, you can show them your essay plans. They will be able to judge almost at a glance whether a plan leaves out anything which ought to be in, whether it is reasonably logically constructed, and whether the essay would answer the question in the way they want.
- Third, your essay plans will help you identify gaps in the material that you have at your disposal. Once you've got your plan, check that you have material to put under each of your headings and subheadings. If you haven't, or haven't enough, then you need to go looking for it.

If you're in the situation where exams are looming and you need to find material quickly, your search has to be as well targeted as you can make it. So you need to be as clear as possible about what it is that you need, and to have a systematic and efficient approach to finding it. Whatever you have to consult – books, lecture handouts, your own notes – try to avoid plodding page by page through them. Thus, if you're working with a book, first check out chapter headings and subheadings and the index for mentions of your target material, then do the same by scanning the introductory and concluding chapters. If the concluding chapter doesn't actually contain the author's conclusions (as is not infrequently the case with academic books), look for these in the introduction and the final parts of individual chapters.

Bear in mind that if you have three or four essays to write in three hours the number of words you'll be putting on to paper will be in the hundreds. The average book of 250 pages contains about 100,000 words. A meaty article in a journal will have 5000–15,000 words. So you simply won't be able to reproduce or paraphrase sizeable chunks of a publication. Unless a single book or article will be the subject of a question, you need only main points, possibly to do with principles or the 'gist' of the work, backed up by two or three telling details. Direct your search towards these: don't try to ingest and digest massive quantities of stuff.

Box 4

Make good use of revision sessions

If your teachers hold revision sessions – seminars, classes or tutorials – you *must* attend these. On no account miss them. They can be of immense value to you.

Teachers may use revision sessions for a number of purposes: to go over material covered during the year, to demonstrate exam technique using exam questions from past papers, to warn you against common errors, to answer your questions and clear up any misconceptions, and even to give you hints as to topics that might come up in the forthcoming exam. Your teacher may be keen to ensure that there is a 'level playing field' in the sense that all students are given the same pre-exam 'briefing', and a revision session is an opportunity to deliver the same message to everyone. So it's really important to attend.

By all means listen carefully to what you are told and try to take good notes, but there is something more you should do: keep in your mind the question: 'Why is he/she telling us this?' Sometimes the answer will be straightforward: they want you to answer the question as set rather than a different one; they want you to answer the required number of questions, because they would like you to do yourself justice. (And of course good exam results will give the impression that the teaching has been good.)

But sometimes the answer will not be so obvious. Your teacher may deal with a topic not only because you have covered it in the syllabus but also because it is going to come up in the exam, or may use or repeat an unusual word because it features in a question on the exam paper. You may be given a warning that in fact relates to a question. Or your teacher may deal with something very cursorily because it is *not* going to come up.

So: why is your teacher telling you this? Keep an eye open for signs. Listen out for clues. Read between the lines. There is almost always more than meets the eye.

Memorizing

The purpose of revising is to enable you, when you see the actual questions on the exam paper in front of you, to reach into your mind and gain access to the thoughts, words, sentences, sounds, pictures and feelings stored there. Thus effective revising involves not only learning but also *memorizing*. It's helpful to regard memorizing as having two components: (a) installing thoughts etc. in your mind: putting them on your mental shelves, so to speak; and (b) making them easy to retrieve: making it easy to locate the shelves holding the stuff you need so you can easily reach up and fetch it down. 'Installing' and 'retrieving': remember these! Bear in mind that when it comes to exams there's no point in installing stuff if you can't retrieve it. So you need to pay attention to both.

I urged you in the previous section not to think of revising, or reviewing, as a matter of cramming into your head as much stuff as possible. If you do that, you risk turning your mind into a dark attic crammed with junk rather than an airy, well-lit larder with goodies neatly arranged on the shelves. Retrieving what you want from a dark attic crammed with junk, under exam conditions, is really hard. So don't try to cram, especially in the last few days before an exam. Instead, spend that time on visiting your larder, reminding yourself where everything is to be found: on which shelf, which items are next to one another, and so on.

When exams are more than a couple of weeks away, you still have time to do some installing. Here are some thoughts about how to do it:

- Limit your task. Divide it into sub-tasks, and aim to complete each one before going on to the next. Check that you've completed it (a) by seeing if you can answer a question on the material; or (b) by putting the material to one side and asking yourself: 'What are the main points I've got from this?'
- Make revision notes. Redo notes that you've made during the semester or year. Copy them out in 'minimalist' form: think of this not as condensing but as stripping out everything but the essentials. (Condensed material tends to be highly indigestible!) Compartmentalize and cross-check: look out for common features and interconnections. And add any new material that's relevant and that you can just slot into place. Incidentally, it's most unlikely that 'non-essentials' will be lost to you. The chances are that your subconscious mind will register them and have them ready for you if you need them in the exam. (Just as your peripheral vision registers words or objects within your vision even if you don't look at them directly.)
- Relate new stuff to what you already know. The stuff you have already serves as a kind of Velcro to which new stuff will stick. So link it in: cross-check, categorize, compare and contrast with what you already have. Ask yourself: 'Does this new stuff fit into the bigger picture? Do I need to alter the bigger picture?'
- Draw up essay plans or 'bullet point' answers to questions on past exam papers. By doing this you are formulating material in a different way from that in which you first encountered it, in written form or in lectures, and this – as well as preparing you for the exam itself – will help the installing process.

- Spend a little time each morning going over the work you did the day before. This will help to reinforce yesterday's work before today's work entirely replaces it in your conscious mind.
- Test yourself, or – better still – get someone to test you. This is something well worth doing with friends, people you trust. It's not only a way of revealing any gaps in your knowledge and reasoning: the process of articulating – expressing in words – your knowledge and thoughts will usually have the twofold effect of clarifying them and at the same time embedding them in your mind. This comes about because the way we write is not the way we speak. Try reading out one of your essays to your friends: you'll find yourself using simpler expressions, and 'unpacking' complex sentences into the various statements that make them up.

All these installing activities involve intellectual effort. You might find that you're talking to yourself a lot. Don't worry! That's perfectly normal.

At the same time as installing material in your 'larder', you have to give some thought to retrieving it later. Here are some thoughts for facilitating retrieval:

- It will help you a great deal if your larder is neat and well organized. This requires that both the shelves and the goodies on them are clearly labelled. It will help you to recollect what is there if the labels are distinctive, and if you put some effort into creating them, because you will have memories of that creative activity. So if you've been doing a basic economics course, say, make sure your macroeconomics notes and your microeconomics notes are in separate folders, of different colours, and clearly labelled:

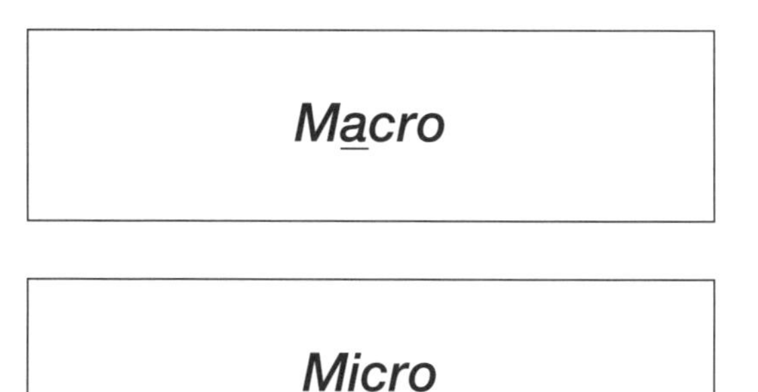

- Make your revision notes visually memorable. Remember, you want your mind to be like an airy, well-lit larder with goodies clearly labelled and neatly arranged on the shelves, not like a dark attic crammed with junk. So leave plenty of space on the page: wide margins, space between paragraphs. Use coloured pens, coloured paper, highlighters, Post-its of different colours. Some people find 'mind maps' work very well but not everybody does, so experiment before committing yourself to this technique.
- Make lists and tables. These are excellent for encapsulating a lot of material and seeing it at a glance. You may well find that you like having your list or table in a box (i.e. with a border round it): do experiment! When you're happy with your list or table – but not before – run your finger slowly down the list and read out aloud the writing in each row as you come to it. Now take one or more highlighters and colour in the backgrounds to the various rows. You could leave alternate ones blank or you could use the full range of colours available to you.
- Draw diagrams and sketches. If you're dealing with linked sequences of any kind – for example, steps in reasoning, chronological sequences – use diagrams and sketches to make these visual. Use boxes (which can be of different shapes and colours) and connect them up by lines (which again can be of different kinds, e.g. continuous or dotted) with arrow-heads to denote directionality.
- When you've put something on paper, sit back, take a look at it, then try to picture it in your mind's eye. If you're right-handed, you might find this easier if you direct your eyes upwards and to the left, even if your eyes are closed: if you're left-handed, try looking upwards and to the right. If you do this with your eyes open, it works better if you're looking in the direction of a piece of blank wall rather than towards something that could distract you. Take your time, breathe steadily and deeply, and alternately look at the picture in your mind's eye and the paper in your hand or on your table. Compare the two. Check that the picture in your mind's eye is the same as the writing and diagrams etc. on the paper. When you've got a good match, you're done. Even people who think they have a poor visual sense can do this with a bit of practice.

- Make fresh copies of revision notes you've already made. Both the repetition and the very act of copying will make it easier to recollect these later.
- When you're making notes, say the words aloud or under your breath as you write. If you have a list of points, recite them like a poem.
- Play word games. These act as mnemonics, aids to memory. Use patterns of words, lists of initial letters, and so on. The sentence 'Richard Of York Gave Battle In Vain' has long been used to remind British school-children that the colours of the spectrum are Red, Orange, Yellow, Green, Blue, Indigo, Violet. Make up your own sentences. Playing word games like these will help to give you a feeling of pleasure and familiarity when you use them in an exam.
- Some people like to make 'cue cards' for themselves: file cards with just a few words on them to act as reminders, or 'triggers', intended to evoke fuller recollections of material. Be careful with this one, though. I have known one or two students who found in the exam that they could remember the cue card perfectly but nothing that lay behind it, as if the cue card were blocking everything else out. So try this method out before committing yourself to it.

As I'm sure you can by now appreciate, when it comes to making your materials as easy to retrieve as possible, the principle is twofold: (a) to make full use of your senses, especially your eyes and ears and your sense of touch and movement; and (b) to use *all* your senses if you can. You may think of yourself as primarily visual or auditory or kinaesthetic, and by all means play to your strengths, but you are likely to derive maximum benefit from using all of your senses rather than using only your best. Experiment! Find out what works for you.

▼ ▼ ▼

Note: There are specialist books on developing and using your memory, and on mind maps. See 'Further reading' for details of some sources.

Box 5

If you become ill or there's a family emergency

If you become ill or there's a family emergency during the run-up to exams, or during the exam period itself, and you wish to have this taken into account by the examiners, it is crucial to get medical evidence from your doctor or evidence about the emergency from someone of professional standing. Preferably this will be someone who can say with some authority how your exam preparation has been affected. Find out who this evidence should be sent to – this could be an administrator or the person who chairs the relevant examination board – and make sure it reaches them. You *must* make a photocopy before letting it out of your possession, in case the original goes missing.

Add a covering letter from yourself giving your own account of the circumstances and how they have affected your ability to do yourself justice in the exams. If you have got good marks for your coursework during the year or semester, it can do you no harm to mention these in your letter. It's best not to assume that this information will be available to the examination board when it meets.

The purpose of doing all this is of course to ensure that the circumstances are taken into account by the examiners when they meet to agree marks and degree classes, and take decisions (or make recommendations) about progressing to the next stage of your degree programme. It might influence them in deciding whether to raise a borderline mark, whether to condone poor results in one or two papers, whether you should be permitted to progress into the next year or semester, or whether you should be offered the chance to retake a paper or be examined orally during the vacation.

There is a word of warning that I must put in here. Most examiners will be sympathetic if you have been ill or there has been a family emergency, but there are limits on how far they can take such circumstances into account. The limit has been reached when they start thinking: 'Hang on a minute! We give degrees for academic achievement, not for illness or hardship!' If there is scant evidence of academic achievement on your part, there will be little that they can do.

Make best use of your time

An important prerequisite for making the best use of your time is to keep up your motivation. In the run-up to exams just about everyone finds their motivation going up and down. The downs usually come about through a combination of factors: typically the feeling that you have a mountain to climb to do all the necessary preparation, the pressure to fulfil social or family duties, and sheer tiredness.

The suggestions made in the previous two sections for revising effectively and memorizing should help you to restore your motivation by breaking down your overall task into many small ones: in effect, breaking down the mountain into a collection of molehills. Make a list (or lists) of these small tasks, group related ones together and tick them off as you tackle them, and your task will seem much less oppressive.

Once you know when your exams are, it becomes much easier to plan for them. You've got to have the calendar for the 'run-up' period crystal clear in your mind. Make a calendar, with a space for notes by each day, and put it up on your wall, so it becomes part of your scenery. Mark your exam dates on it, and any other crucial dates you need to be aware of.

Do everything you can to clear the decks for exam preparation. It's important to eliminate so far as possible all distractions. If your birthday comes during this period put off your party until your exams are over. Get someone to help you with household duties, make sure you have time for yourself and that your family members and friends understand the need for it and respect it. Now is not a good time to have to listen to other people's woes. If you have a part-time job, organize a holiday from it. If you're invited for a job interview, again, try to get it postponed until after exams. If you have a dissertation to write and hand in after your exams, and it's preying on your mind, draw up a rough plan for it for yourself and jot down whatever thoughts you have about it. It will probably hang around at the back of your mind and every now and again ideas for developing it and adding to it will pop into your head – just make a note of them – but you are unlikely to be troubled by it.

Work out how many days you have available altogether for preparation. This will be the number of days from today until your last exam, minus the number of days on which you are actually sitting exams and minus the number of days you require for essential time off. Divide the number of available days by the number of exams you're taking, to find the average number of days you have available per subject. (This should get your adrenaline going. If it doesn't, choose one of your courses and divide the number of days available for it by the number of topics you want to revise. That should stimulate the requisite sense of urgency in you.)

Look at your exam timetable. Do your exams cluster together in a solid block, or are they spread out? If you discover they're in a solid block – perhaps even morning and afternoon on successive days – be aware that there are some advantages to this. You won't be tempted to devote a disproportionate amount of time to your first exam, and because of the proximity of your next exam you're unlikely to be spending any time between exams reflecting on those that you have just taken.

Whether your exams cluster or not, look at your calendar and do some planning. Think about how many days, and what proportion of the total number of days that you have available, you need for each of your subjects.

(It's probably best to allocate whole days, otherwise your programme is liable to become rather bitty and get out of control.) Make a 'to-do' list for each of your subjects, and keep these lists under review. Tick items off as you deal with them. Every day, when you start work, do so with a list for that day.

One approach is to start by preparing your 'best' subjects, to clear the decks for getting on with the others. Alternatively, if there's one subject that is causing you particular concern, you may want to start with that one, but select just a few topics to work on, to get your anxiety under control. Don't let that subject eat up all your time. Once you've got going, even after you switch to another subject your mind will keep puzzling away at the difficult things. (Minds do this: your mind has a mind of its own.)

As I said earlier, don't feel you have to cram more and more stuff into your head. If you have spent all day in the library copying out stuff or cudgelling your brain to condense an author's words into tightly packed paragraphs, you have pretty much wasted the day. But if you spent an hour working out exactly what material you needed and another hour extracting it from your sources and slotting it into place in your essay plans, you have accomplished far more, and in a fraction of the time.

And please do your best to avoid getting bogged down in whatever you're doing. If you spend even half an hour getting nowhere, you are not making good use of your time. Step back and figure out a different approach. Try to work out what the difficulty is, and make a note of it. Get out the Post-its. Get hold of a different book. Talk to a fellow student. Phone a friend. Switch to another subject for the rest of the day. Give yourself a break from work. Whatever you do, develop a range of strategies for circumventing obstacles.

If you do come across a book that you feel you *must* read, and are tempted to resort to anxious, stomach-tightening note taking, try a different approach. Try relaxing into it! Find a really comfortable and well-lit place, equip yourself with a supply of chocolate, and some Post-its in case you want to bookmark some passages, and just let yourself browse through the book. Playing baroque orchestral music could help. (Handel, Vivaldi, Bach, Corelli and Telemann are recommended.) When you've read the relevant bits, close the book, take a pen and paper (and some slow, deep breaths) and just jot down whatever comes into your mind about what you've read. When you're relaxed, your subconscious mind comes into play, and you may be very pleasantly surprised by the amount of learning it does for you.

We all have our own body rhythms and preferred work patterns. You ought to know at what times of day, and under what conditions, you work best. When you're preparing for exams, try to work 'with the grain'. Try to get the sleep, the food and the exercise you need, when you need them. If you're an 'evening person', however, it may be an idea to try to advance your daily timetable a little each day, since exams aren't (usually) held in the evening. Don't give yourself a hard time; don't force a punishing schedule on yourself. Your adrenaline will help you get by on less sleep and food than the ideal, but probably not for days and certainly not for weeks on end, and if your schedule is too demanding your performance will suffer.

Box 6

Avoid getting wound up by other students!

Some people are very skilled at making others feel insecure. At exam time we are particularly vulnerable to this. If you find you're getting 'wound up' by someone, avoid that person's company. It isn't good for you. Don't get hooked into spending time or – especially – having meals with him or her. (It's not good for your digestion.) Stay away!

If you know that there isn't a formula or quota system governing how many Firsts, Upper Seconds, Lower Seconds, etc. (or distinctions and merits in the case of Master's students) are awarded, you will know that you are not competing against your fellow students. Hang out with people who don't have to score points off you to feel good themselves.

Box 7

Practise writing legibly

How legible is your handwriting? If you normally use a computer/word processor for writing essays and letters, you probably have little incentive to make your handwriting easy for other people to read. (The notion of the 'fair copy' seems to have died out some years ago.) Indeed, if most of the writing you do consists of making notes in lectures, your handwriting may have turned into a kind of shorthand that only you can read.

But in 2004 it is still the norm under the traditional exam system that you write out your answers by hand, into the answer books provided. These answers have then to be read by the examiners, so it is important that they be legible. (The rise of the word-processed essay has meant not only that students' handwriting has become more difficult to read, but also that teachers' skill at deciphering it has become rusty.) If the examiners can't read your handwriting, it is possible that you could lose marks or even fail the paper. In some places there may be provision for a candidate to be called back and required to dictate his or her answers to a typist, at the candidate's own expense. (But don't bank on this facility being available to you.)

So do this. Take a book and copy out a page, writing as quickly as you can. Then show it to friends whose judgment you can trust and see if they can read it. Get them to tell you which words they can't decipher and identify the problems. It may be that certain pairs of letters are indistinguishable – 'a' and 'o', or 'n' and 'u', for example – or that certain letters aren't fully formed – 't' left uncrossed, 'i' left undotted – or that your up-strokes (on 'b', 'd', 'f', 'h', 'k', 'l', 't') and down-strokes (on 'g', 'j', 'p', 'q', 'y') aren't long enough. Then copy out another page from the book, paying attention to these problems, and try this one out on your friends. You should find you've made a significant improvement.

Keep practising your improved handwriting – when redoing your notes, for example – and you should find that you're soon back at your original speed, or even writing faster.

It's also worth experimenting with different pens. If you're accustomed to using a ballpen, you may find that some of the modern, more free-flowing pens enable you to write faster. They also require less pressure, so they're less tiring to use.

Getting in the right frame of mind for exams

How successful you are in your exams depends on a number of things. It depends on how much work you have done during the year or semester towards mastering your subjects; on how effectively you have revised, memorized and used your time in the run-up to the exams; and on getting in the right frame of mind for exams.

Getting in the right frame of mind is crucial. I've known hard-working, conscientious students say things like 'I'm afraid I won't remember the stuff I need when I'm in the exam room.' I've always been sure that if anything were to get in the way of their doing well it would be the *fear* of not remembering, rather than an inability to remember.

Anything that you have paid attention to and worked on will be on a shelf in your mind: your subconscious mind if not your conscious one. Fear makes it more difficult to retrieve that material. (Fright can paralyse, as everyone knows.) In contrast, being relaxed makes it easier to retrieve stuff. You must have had the experience of solutions to problems popping into your head spontaneously when you're relaxed and thinking about something else. While taking an exam isn't conducive to quite that level of relaxation, there *are* things you can do – beforehand and in the exam itself – that will help you to get into the state of mind that will enable you to do justice to yourself and to the work that you have done during the year or semester.

So here are some suggestions. Essentially they are mental exercises. They require nothing by way of equipment, only a quiet place where you can be on your own, and they require you to disclose nothing about yourself to other people. All are perfectly do-able: tried and tested and found to work.

Don't label yourself

First of all, don't label yourself. Don't say things like: 'I'm someone who panics in exams.' Labels are self-fulfilling. The more that you tell yourself that you're someone who panics in exams, the more difficult you're making it for yourself *not* to panic in exams! If you label yourself as someone who panics, you are shutting off strategies for not panicking: in effect you're saying to yourself: 'Strategies for panicking are useless to me!'

It may be that in the past you have indeed experienced panic. I'm not trying to rewrite your history. But the past is past. You're not doomed to repeat it if you don't want to. Please open your mind to the possibility that you could actually do rather well this time round.

Envisage success

Prophecies, like labels, are often self-fulfilling. If you anticipate problems, you will certainly have problems. You'll be on the look-out for them, you'll tune in to them, they'll jump out at you.

So, anticipate success instead. Then it'll be ways of achieving success that spring to your attention. If an athlete started a race with his or her mind focused on 'problems', it would not be conducive to winning. It's the same for you. Envisage success! Go and take a look if you can at the room that you'll be sitting the exam in. Then run a movie of yourself sitting in the exam room creating essay plans and contentedly covering the pages of your answer book. You could even 'step into' the movie and start writing! It will certainly make working for exams more pleasurable if there are some pleasurable feelings associated with it.

I appreciate that you may not find this easy at first. Perhaps you had it dinned into you as a child: 'Don't count your chickens before they've hatched.' Recognize that you were being actively taught not to envisage success. It's a completely counter-productive message, of course: there's no better incentive to taking good care of eggs than the prospect of getting a chicken from each one. So, instead, envisage yourself actively helping eggs to hatch and taking pleasure in the results!

Access your resources

What state of mind do you want to be in? Calm, confident, determined, competent, alert, creative, motivated, able to concentrate, . . .? (Make your own list.) Calmness, confidence etc. are resources. The object of this exercise is to enable you to gain access to these resources whenever you want to do so.

Now, remember an occasion in the past when you were calm and determined. (Yes, of course you have experienced such an occasion in the past, many times, or you wouldn't be where you are today.) You had the resources then, so gaining access to them now involves 'recapturing' them in some way.

Here is one way of achieving that recapturing. Take yourself back to that occasion: that time, that place . . . See again in your mind's eye what you saw then; hear again what you heard then; experience again the feelings that you felt then. Notice who and what is in the picture, what sounds are reaching your ears, what the feelings are that you're experiencing. Now come back to the present: move about and give yourself a little shake of arms and legs to 'break state'.

Next, you're going to do the equivalent of tying a knot in your handkerchief to remind you of the resourceful state. Choose a small gesture, like pressing two fingers together, or placing your hand firmly on your knee.

Now take yourself back to that occasion once more, to the resourceful state you were in then. Once more, see again what you were seeing then; hear again the sounds that you heard then; and let yourself experience again the feelings that you felt then. When that feeling of being calm and determined is with you again, and you're really into it, make the gesture and hold it while the feeling lasts. When the intensity of the feeling seems to be about to peak, release the gesture. Then have a little shake again and come back to the present.

Repeat these steps several times. You can do this with the same past resourceful occasion or different ones, with the same or different feelings. Soon you will become aware of a strong connection between the gesture and the feelings. You may find that the connection becomes even stronger if, each time you make the gesture, you repeat a particular word or phrase.

Hey presto! You now have a reminder, or 'trigger', for those resources: press the trigger and they will be available to you whenever you want them. And you can take your resources to future situations, before they happen. Imagine yourself in the examination room: see, hear and feel yourself there. Then, using your trigger, invoke your resources: see, hear and feel yourself with those resources there for you.

Banish the voices

Do you hear voices? Can you hear a little voice telling you not to count your chickens, or a little voice telling you ' "I want" doesn't get'? If you let the latter message get to you, you are effectively denying yourself the right, the entitlement, to have personal objectives.

You don't need this stuff. What to do? Use your imagination. Try repeating the message in the voice of a cartoon character (Donald Duck?) or a really dim politician. Raise the pitch until it's really squeaky. Try accompanying it with an orchestra or heavy metal group playing really loudly. Each time you hear the voice imagine that it's coming from your radio, and imagine turning the volume control steadily down and down and down and down ... and finally put out your hand and switch the radio off altogether, saying 'Click' as you do so. Sounds weird? Do it a number of times and you will have learned to associate the nagging voice with ridicule and a sense of your own power. You'll only need to put out your hand and say 'Click' and the voice will turn off and let you get on with your work. Top sportspeople do this to improve their performance: you can too.

Are you good at worrying? Worrying is nothing more than an extremely effective way of conjuring up disaster scenarios. If pictures come into your mind of situations you'd rather not be in, use your imagination to deal with them. See them reflected in a distorting mirror. If they're in colour, turn people's faces lime green or beetroot red, or put the whole picture into black and white. Put the picture in a frame, and tilt the frame away from you or turn it upside down. Experiment until you find a way of handling the images that takes away their power to make you feel threatened.

If you get sound and vision, what you've got is a movie. Run it very very quickly, first forwards and then backwards. Or play it as a video on a portable TV: put the TV on the back of a truck and as the truck drives off watch it get smaller and smaller and smaller and smaller and listen to the sound get quieter and quieter and quieter and quieter, and wave it goodbye as it disappears round a corner taking picture and sound with it.

Unstick yourself from the past

Maybe, like just about everyone else, from time to time you're afflicted with uncomfortable or even painful memories of past situations you've been in. At stressful times, like when you're working for exams, you're more likely to be vulnerable to these. The memory may be so 'real' that you feel as though you're there again, in the same time and place, and with the same people. When it's so real that you can't tell past from present, what's happening is that you're thoroughly stuck in that past experience. What to do? Get some practice at unsticking yourself. Here's something you can do.

First, imagine yourself in a past painful situation. Take yourself back to whenever it was. Briefly remind yourself of what you were seeing then, what you were hearing, and how you felt. Then come back to the present (don't spend longer than you need in painfully recollecting the past!), stand up, give your arms and legs a little shake, one by one, and go and sit in a different chair.

Now imagine that in the chair you've just vacated is sitting a younger you, you as you were in that past situation. Tell that younger you that the future does hold good things, and that that younger you has *ability* – the ability to learn, the ability to move on, the ability to avoid being trapped by people and situations from the past, and especially the ability to learn and to do things differently in the future. Use your own words, of course.

Be objective!

Another good stance to have available is 'objective you'. (Yes, another chair in the room would come in handy!) This is the position from which you take a detached look at 'you now'. You observe how interesting it is that 'you now' are carrying with you these feelings and behaviour patterns from the past, and you ask questions like 'What is there to be learned from past experiences?' and 'Are my feelings appropriate to "me now" or are they feelings that belong to "me then"?'

Taking a questioning approach like this to past and present experiences and situations helps you to stand outside them. It helps you to separate yourself from 'you then' and also from 'you now', especially valuable when those two positions are fused, when 'you now' is reliving a painful past. And if you find yourself consistently being 'dumped on' – as when someone else shares their bad feelings with you and you find yourself feeling bad as a result – then ask yourself whether it's appropriate to allow that to happen. Questioning helps you to extricate yourself and thus to maintain your own balance.

Incidentally, persistently asking what there is to be learned from your experiences will have a valuable extra benefit. It'll remind you that 'There is no failure, only feedback.'

Choose a new perspective

You can give yourself a choice of perspectives from which to view exams. If you normally view exams as an ordeal, try switching to another view. Think of them instead as an opportunity to write about a subject without having to grind out a 1500-word essay, dealing with the subject completely and comprehensively and replete with quotations scrupulously reproduced and references punctiliously documented.

Instead you can show that you have a 'bird's eye' overview of the subject, that you have an eye for discrepancies in the literature you have read, that you can use specific cases to test generalizations, that there are interesting things that you have noticed and thought about and tried to make sense of, that you can formulate a structured and systematic approach to questions, and so on. These are all skills that you have been acquiring over the year: think of exams as an opportunity to demonstrate them.

Develop the strategies you already have

If you have an unhelpful amount of anxiety as exams approach, it is probably not helpful to focus your energy on discovering why you have it. The effect may well be that you install it more firmly than ever: you're now giving yourself reasons for being anxious! So don't do that! Instead, ask what the steps are by which you get into an anxious state. When you get anxious, do you tell yourself about past bad times? Then what you have is a strategy for getting into and staying in an anxious state, a strategy which consists of tapping into memories of past bad times and telling yourself about them. Try something different!

In effect, the mental exercises described above are strategies for getting into good, resourceful states. So try them out. And do remember that you've had past experiences of being in a good state and you'll have them in the future. Next time you're in a good, resourceful state, notice it, and notice the steps by which you got into it. What did you see, what did you say to yourself, what did you feel; and in what order? Then repeat those steps consciously, and practise them as required. Find what it is that acts as a good reminder of it for you – the knot in the handkerchief again – and consciously use that too. You now have your very own, custom-made, feel-good strategy. Remember: you have the capacity to do all this for yourself!

And there's more. You can experiment by amending your strategies, by trying variations. You could change one of the steps, or the order of the steps. Or you can identify a step where there's a choice to do something different and aim for a different result. Try it!

Find yourself a good metaphor

It is often helpful to have a metaphor for yourself, or a 'bit' of yourself. Do you ever think of yourself as a cat or other animal, or a tree (oak? willow?), or a mythical figure, or something constructed, like a pyramid or a ship? Would you like to have a bit of you that's like one of those little dolls with a hemispherical base that always comes upright again after being knocked sideways? The value of metaphors like these is that they help to remind you of your own integrity, and to remind you that fundamentally your worth and self-respect do not depend on your ability to jump through the hoops that academics set for you.

▼ ▼ ▼

Note: These exercises are taken/developed from a field of endeavour known as Neuro-Linguistic Programming (NLP). Defined by the experts as 'the study of the structure of subjective experience', it is more easily thought of as the study and application of the mechanisms by which our experiences affect us and by which we react to them and organize our behaviour. These are mechanisms that involve thinking and feeling, using language, and doing: hence the 'neuro', the 'linguistic' and the 'programming'. See 'Further reading' for details of some sources.

Box 8

Get the sleep you need

After you've been working hard all day preparing for exams, you may find it difficult to switch off. You go to bed, try to sleep, but thoughts keep buzzing around in your brain. What to do? Here are four suggestions.

- Give yourself some 'buffer time' between ending work for the day and going to bed. Watch some TV; do something creative; make yourself a hot, caffeine-free drink; take some exercise, if only press-ups or running up and down the stairs a few times.
- When you get into bed, do some relaxing exercises. Basically these involve tensing then relaxing every muscle you can find in your body. Start by turning up your toes as far as you can, hold for a few seconds,

then relax, letting them go limp. Then turn your toes down and arch your feet as tightly as you can, hold, then relax again. Now turn your feet up as far as you can, and feel your ankles and calves tighten: hold, then relax. Repeat the tense/hold/relax sequence progressively up your body: thighs, bottom, stomach, chest, shoulders. Then fingers, hands, wrists, elbows, shoulders. Then neck, jaw, facial and scalp muscles to finish.

- Here's another exercise. It's very simple. You have to breathe in deeply, and exhale fully (pulling in your stomach), and count your breaths as you do so. Say to yourself (under your breath) 'And' as you breathe in, then 'One' as you breathe out. Again, say 'And' as you breathe in, then 'Two' as you breathe out. And so on. When you lose count of the number you're up to, start again at 'One'. For an added refinement, picture a computer screen, and every time you breathe out, picture the cursor clicking on the little x in the top right-hand corner and the screen going blank.
- Finally, keep a notepad and pencil by your bedside. If thoughts persist in coming into your mind, write them down. Then you can relax, knowing they'll be there for you in the morning.

Part Four

On the day of the exam

Be organized

Turn up!

Do, *do* turn up to the examination. Failure to do so can have serious consequences. If you oversleep, or your train is delayed, nevertheless do your best to get to the examination room as soon as possible, and at all costs before the examination has finished and people come out carrying the exam paper. If you've been given a phone number to call in an emergency, make sure you have a note of it on you or that you've programmed it into your (charged-up) mobile phone.

What to take

Take with you whatever form you have been given that tells you which building and room you should go to, and what your personal candidate number is. Leave yourself enough time to find the room and then the desk allocated to you. (There should be a plan outside the examination room for you to consult.)

Make sure you take a pen with you, plus one or even two spares. If you're taking a calculator, make sure the battery is well charged.

If you are permitted to take food or drink into the examination room, and you feel you really must, then as a matter of courtesy and fairness to other candidates make sure they are such that you can open them and consume them noiselessly, so other people aren't distracted.

When you get there

You should already have been informed what materials will be supplied and on your desk ready for you, and what you are allowed to bring in with you (e.g. calculator, reference materials).

You will be required to leave any bag that you have with you by the door, as you enter the room. To avoid the possibility of embarrassing misunderstandings, make very sure you do not take any unauthorized material (e.g. your revision notes) with you to your desk.

Answer books

On your desk you will find a blank answer book. You should already have been told what you have to write on the front cover: for example, your candidate number, the title (and possibly the code number, if any) of the exam paper, maybe the date, maybe details of any calculator you've been permitted to bring in and use.

There may also be, on the front of the answer book, instructions and warnings about how you are to use it: for example 'Write legibly' and 'Start every answer on a new page.' You should have been told all of these in advance: there should be nothing new for you to digest and adapt to.

You should use the answer book for your essay plans and any other 'rough working' as well as for your answers. Simply draw a diagonal line through anything that you don't want the examiners to read.

The invigilator (supervisor) will supply you with additional answer books when you need them. Just put your hand up when you're getting towards the end of one.

The exam paper

Read the 'rubric' – the instructions – on the front cover of the exam paper. Read these instructions carefully, and check them again after each question you've tackled. Note how many questions you have to answer. Some papers are divided into sections, and you *must* note and follow the instructions. For example, if a paper is divided into two sections and the rubric says 'Answer three questions, at least one question from Section A and one from Section B', that is exactly what you must do. The instructions don't tell you which section your third question is to be drawn from, so you have a choice. Hence you will be complying with the instructions if you answer two questions from Section A and one from Section B, or if you answer one question from Section A and two from Section B.

Read the exam questions through, carefully. (In some subjects you will have some 'reading time' at the beginning to do this.) Make sure you don't miss any pages, and do look at both sides of each sheet. You will feel unhappy if, after the exam is over, you come out of the examination room and suddenly realize there was a question on the paper that you could have done but didn't notice.

Among other things, reading the paper through will show you how the examiners have divided up the subject, and give you some clues about how to answer the questions. For example, if in a government and politics paper there is one question on policy-making and another on pressure groups, and you want to answer both, do not write at length about pressure groups in your answer on policy-making, and vice versa. Don't write the same answer, or part-answer, to two questions.

It is extremely rare for a mistake to be made in producing an exam paper, but I have known it to happen. If you believe a question is incomplete or does not make sense, put your hand up to attract the invigilator's attention and quietly point out the problem. He or she will call for assistance if they think it appropriate. (That is the limit of their responsibility: they cannot give you any help in understanding a question.) Candidates will not be penalized if examiners realize, when they come to mark scripts, that a question has been badly worded.

Your general strategy

Some people like to hold 'easy' questions in reserve, but you may prefer to start with a question that you feel well-equipped to answer, a strategy that is also likely to give you confidence and dispel nerves. There is another reason for doing this. If the exam is disrupted – for example, if a fire alarm goes off and the building has to be evacuated – it will have to be terminated. It could be that candidates affected will have their scripts marked as they stand and the mark then scaled up. Examination boards will doubtless be sympathetic, but you may wish to minimize your dependence on sympathy.

Do answer the required number of questions. If you answer only three out of four (say) on an undergraduate paper, even if they are all of middle Upper Second quality, simple arithmetic may dictate that your mark overall for the paper is only a Third. So do your best to keep to time. If you do find that you've left yourself only 15 or 20 minutes for your fourth question, an answer in note form – putting down the salient points, one per paragraph – will salvage a few marks for you, possibly making the difference between – say – an Upper Second and a Lower Second.

Your answers will not necessarily be marked in the order in which you write them. So in answering one question, don't refer to answers that you've already given to others.

And if you are answering two questions where there is a certain amount of 'overlap' of the subject matter, do your best not to use the same material in both your answers.

Either/or questions: answer the (a) question or the (b) question, but *not both*. (Occasionally, under the stress of the situation, candidates have done this.) Usually, questions are bracketed in this way because there is some overlap between them. So if you choose to answer the (a) question, the (b) question may give you some ideas about what to put in your answer and/or how to structure it.

Don't begin an answer by writing: 'Before answering the question ...'. There is *nothing* you should write (that you want the examiners to read) before answering the question.

Try not to repeat yourself. As I said earlier, you gain no extra marks for writing something twice.

Time is of course limited, and you will want to write as quickly as you can, but do your best to write legibly. (See Box 7 on page 78.) If you think your writing will be easier to read if you write on alternate lines, you ought to be able to do this without being penalized. I doubt whether you will find in the exam regulations anything to the effect that extravagant use of answer books is an examination offence. And however legible your handwriting, leave a blank line between each paragraph. It will make your answers easier to read, and the examiners will be grateful.

Even if you aren't specifically required to do so, start each of your answers on a new page of your answer book. You may well find the space left at the end of an answer useful for inserting afterthoughts.

For the same reason, leave two or three lines at the foot of each page for inserting afterthoughts as footnotes.

It is usually acceptable to use abbreviations (check beforehand with your teachers), but make it clear what they stand for. For example, the first time you write 'local authority', write 'LA' in brackets after it. Thereafter, use 'LA' as your abbreviation. Likewise, 'Government' can become 'Govt', 'Prime Minister' 'PM', and so on.

Answering the question

This is where all the practice you've had at formulating answers really pays dividends. Remember the list of points to cover in drawing up a plan, set out in Checklist 10 on page 42 –

- *Introduction*
  Context/background
  Interpretation
  Methodology
  Materials
  Outline of following sections
- *Findings, Reasoning/analysis* and *Results* (but use headings appropriate to your subject and material)
- *Discussion*
- *Conclusions*

– and use it to start piecing your answer together. Don't dive straight into the subject. Pay particular attention to interpretation, because that will help to ensure that you stick to the question and don't deviate from it. And think about the methodology you will use. A systematic approach will gain you more marks than the ability to reproduce large chunks of text that you have memorized. (You have to have some knowledge, of course, but most degree-level exams are not memory tests.) And slot in under 'Discussion' any interesting points that come to mind which you think will 'add value' to your answer, even if you can't get them to flow neatly.

If you feel yourself starting to panic . . .

Finally . . . what to do if you feel yourself starting to panic. Breathe!!! If you are feeling anxious during an exam (or indeed at any other time), slow your breathing rate and take your time to exhale. If you exhale rapidly carbon dioxide can build up in your bloodstream, and that will produce symptoms of anxiety. Indeed, it is possible to make yourself feel anxious by hyper-ventilating: i.e. breathing quickly and shallowly as if you were frightened. So do the opposite. Breathe as you would do if you were relaxed. Breathe out slowly and fully: this will ensure that you take deep breaths too (and the oxygen will also help you burn up the excess adrenaline you'll be generating). Acting as if you feel good – breathing steadily, sitting in a relaxed but alert fashion, even smiling to yourself – will start to produce that very feeling.

And cast your mind back to the exercises you did to get in the right frame of mind for exams. Remember the little gesture, your trigger for taking yourself into your resourceful states: pressing two fingers together, or placing your hand firmly on your knee, or something similar. Make that gesture now, and summon up your resources: see yourself as calm and determined; remind (tell) yourself that calmness and determination are still available to you; experience again that feeling of being calm and determined.

Now, choose a question. Start jotting down some rough notes on the subject, and you'll find that you're beginning to unlock your 'larder' and all that stuff on the shelves in your mind. Once you get engrossed in what you're doing you'll forget to panic!

Box 9

After it's all over

After your exams are all over, what will you do? Most people find a spot of celebration is in order. It's almost impossible not to relive the exams a bit, and after an exam just about everybody thinks of something they ought to have put in an answer but didn't. Partying will at least take your mind off those things. And however you feel about how you've done, you have survived, and that should be a cause for celebration.

Try to avoid getting into post-mortems, discussions about the exam papers, what the examiners were looking for, and the brilliant answers that some of your fellow candidates gave. Such discussions are liable to get very excitable and increase the tension you're still feeling. The people who tried to wind you up before exams will probably try to wind you up after them as well, and my advice is the same: keep out of their way. You don't need more tension.

Bear this in mind too: experience shows that after an exam candidates are not in a good position to judge how well they have done. So try not to rerun the exam in your mind. Find something to do that will take your mind off it. Physical activity often works well, especially if you've deprived yourself of exercise during the exam period.

As you know all too well, exams are stressful, and when they're over you may feel very 'flat': a natural consequence of 'adrenaline slump'. So it's a good idea to set aside some recovery time too. If you're sleeping a lot, that's part of the recovery process: don't worry about it.

Finally, let's have a bit of perspective here. I know a lot may be at stake, but the academic world is not the real world. Please do bear in mind what I said earlier: fundamentally your worth and self-respect do not depend on your ability to jump through the hoops that academics set for you.

Box 10

Web links, feedback, updates

Links to useful websites can be found by logging on to

www.student-friendly-guides.com

If you have any questions about preparing for exams that this book hasn't covered, or any suggestions for improving it, please log on to the website and email them to me. I'll be glad to answer any questions, and all suggestions for improvements will be very gratefully received.

And don't forget to check out the website regularly for updates to this and other student-friendly guides.

Further reading

All of these books are published in paperback and were in print in early 2004.

On memory and mind maps, see:

Colin Rose, *Accelerated Learning* (Accelerated Learning Systems 1985). One of the most stimulating books on the subject of memory, deservedly still in print 19 years after it first appeared. Has some fascinating material on how music (especially baroque) can assist learning.

Tony Buzan, *Use Your Memory* (Revised edition, BBC Worldwide 2003). Another long-stayer, first published in 1986. Contains many practical tips.

Tony Buzan and Barry Buzan, *The Mind Map Book* (Revised edition, BBC Worldwide 2003). Comes in two versions: black-and-white, and full colour (recommended). The definitive work on mind maps.

On neuro-linguistic programming (NLP), there are several introductory texts:

Steve Andreas and Charles Faulkner (eds), *NLP: The New Technology of Achievement* (Nicholas Brealey 1996)

Harry Alder and Beryl Heather, *NLP in 21 Days* (Piatkus 1999)

Joseph O'Connor and Ian McDermott, *Way of NLP* (Thorsons 2001)

Joseph O'Connor and John Seymour, *Introducing Neuro-Linguistic Programming* (2nd edition, Element 2002)

Acknowledgments

Many people have contributed, in many different ways, to the birth of this book. I owe a personal thank you to the following people:

The many students who over the years have talked to me about their experiences in higher education: it has been my privilege to work with them.

Penny Tompkins, for her invaluable comments on a draft of the 'Getting in the right frame of mind for exams' section, and Jane Revell and Cricket Kemp: I'm extremely grateful to all three for the assistance and encouragement they have given me in exploring applications of NLP in higher education.

Shona Mullen and her colleagues at the Open University Press, whose understanding, skill, dedication and drive I have every reason to appreciate.

Kate Pool and her colleagues of the Society of Authors, for practical and moral support.

John Levin for his informed comments on early drafts of this book, for the benefit of lessons he learned in the UK higher education system, for his invaluable help with IT and support in the ongoing battle with Dell and Microsoft products, and especially for the pleasure of his company.

Rachel Adriano, who recently re-entered the education system after a very long interval, and whose support for this project I value enormously.

Alice Pizer, for her belief in the importance of my work and writing.

Audrey Cleave, for demonstrating how a youthful, open mind can last and last.

Kevin Fitzgerald and Joe Geraghty, who both know about reinventing themselves: inspirations both.

Clare, Amy and Anne for their affection and encouragement and for road-testing some of the ideas in this book.

Gill, my wife, for her loving care and support, for the memorable times we have together, and for her tolerance (mostly) of a quirky, untidy and often preoccupied author.

Student-Friendly Guides

Successful teamwork!

For undergraduate and taught postgraduate students

This short, practical guide is for students who find themselves placed in groups and assigned a project to carry out.

- Allocating work appropriately
- Dealing with people who are taking a 'free-ride'
- Resolving disagreements
- Working constructively with people who they don't like very much.

The guide helps students to appreciate the tensions between the demands of the task, the needs of the team and individual's needs, and to understand why people behave as they do in a team situation. It provides reassurance when things get stressful, and helps students learn from the experience and make a success of their project.

Contents: Part One: Basics and Context – What do we mean by 'a team'? – The benefits of working in a team – Teamwork skills – Academic teamwork and the job market – Part Two: Getting Started – Get in your groups – Get to know one another – Formulate your ground rules – Check out your assignment and plan your work – Part Three: How are we Doing? – Progress on the project – Progress from 'group' to 'team' – Personal progress – Part Four: Perspectives on Team Behaviour – Tensions: the task, the team and the individual – Team roles – Management systems and team organization – Team development: forming, storming, norming, performing ... – The decision-making process – Negotiation – Cultural traits and differences – Individual traits: 'cats' and 'dogs' – Part Five: Teamwork Issues and Solutions – The task: getting the work done – Personal and inter-personal issues – Part Six: Benefiting from the Experience – Getting feedback – Reflection – Applying for jobs

112pp 0 335 21578 5 (Paperback)